To H/

Trusting this help arrives in time for you to give Hank a decent game now & then.

Best wishes &

John

May 24, 1976

TENNIS
DRILLS

TENNIS DRILLS

On- and Off-Court Drills and Exercises for Beginners, Intermediates, Tournament Players, and Teaching Professionals

BY ROBERT FORD GREENE

Illustrated by Joan Greene
Photographs by Albert Guida
Photographic artwork by Jack Luboff

HAWTHORN BOOKS, INC.
Publishers / New York

TENNIS DRILLS

Library of Congress Catalog Card Number: 75-28689
ISBN: 0-8015-7525-7

1 2 3 4 5 6 7 8 9 10

CONTENTS

SECTION III

DRILLS FOR INTERMEDIATES 69

SECTION IV

ADVANCED AND TOURNAMENT-LEVEL DRILLS

APPENDIX

INDEX

PREFACE

Tennis Drills, the first book devoted to learning and improving tennis exclusively through exercises and drills, is a carefully planned approach to mastery of the game. The drills, in addition to being challenging, enjoyable, and rewarding, will assist both aspiring players and instructors. They are designed for anyone seeking exciting learning experiences through active participation.

For tennis teachers and coaches, ranging from the new instructor to the accomplished teaching professional, the book contains the important steps of teaching the game and lists the key drills sequentially, in order of difficulty. It is also an excellent supplement and workbook for those receiving group or individual tennis instruction. For players and coaches who have limited time available, it offers the most efficient method of practicing. This book is especially helpful for the player or instructor who has limited access to tennis facilities. There are exercises that can be performed in just ten minutes and off-the-court exercises designed to stimulate and accelerate on-the-court improvement.

Tennis Drills will help you attain good form and strokes so that you will not be limited in later years because of improper training. (Once a player establishes poor playing habits with incorrect grips and strokes, it is very difficult—and extremely frustrating—to unlearn them.) This volume promotes the development of all shots, from the touch volley to the bouncing overhead, and includes every exercise necessary to progress from beginner to champion. No step is omitted in the construction of a full arsenal of offensive and defensive weapons. The mixture of these drills with the playing of sets results in an unbeatable combination for learning, improvement, and perfection.

These drills have been thoroughly tested in a multitude of settings by players at all levels. They have been used with outstanding results in individual and group instruction by players ranging from preschool children to senior citizens. Tennis drills are time-savers in becoming a better player.

ACKNOWLEDGMENTS

It gives me great pleasure to thank the following people:

E. Allan Farnsworth, Professor of Law at Columbia University, for suggesting that I record my tennis drills in book form. Originally, I had given him a list of drills to practice with his son, and my pupil, Teddy, a recent New York State twelve-and-under champion.

Bill Berger, my literary agent, for his ability to place the manuscript in the hands of an outstanding publishing house.

Joan B. Nagy, Vice President and Managing Editor of Hawthorn Books, and Bob Oskam, Assistant Editor, for skillfully guiding the manuscript through to publication.

Robert A. Caro, author and good neighbor, who was the first person to see the manuscript and whose initial support meant so much to me.

Steve Gottlieb, Ronald and Jane Rebhuhn, and Dr. Edward Schwartz for reading the manuscript and offering constructive criticism.

Jane and Paul Aronsky for the gracious use of their beautiful court in Kings Point, New York, where most of the photographs were taken.

Captain William "Buck" Lai, Director of Athletics at the United States Merchant Marine Academy in Kings Point, New York, for permission to be photographed at their athletic facility.

Albert Guida, photographer; Jack Luboff, photographic artwork; and Fred Perry, Inc. of New Jersey, for furnishing clothing used in the photographs.

My loving wife and best friend, Joan, for her invaluable assistance in editing and typing, and most importantly, for drawing all of the diagrams that appear in this book.

I wish to dedicate this book to Joan and my family.

Robert Ford Greene
Riverdale, New York
March 1976

INTRODUCTION

The book is divided into three main categories: exercises and drills for beginners, intermediates, and advanced to tournament players. It includes drills specifically planned for rainy days, or when a court is unavailable. A good share of the exercises can be performed alone, without the aid of a partner. Backboard drills are also included.

Many of the exercises are partially programmed, enabling a player to proceed at his own rate of speed. Minimum accuracy standards are often listed so that a player knows when he is sufficiently competent to proceed to the next drill.

"Drills for Beginners" are designed so that the student will use professionally recommended grips and strokes. For those who have never touched a racket, ball and racket familiarization drills are introduced. With this book, parents can have fun starting their children's tennis games in the backyard or playroom of their own home.

"Drills for Intermediates" teach the more difficult shots and reinforce concepts introduced in the beginning section. Control is stressed. Expert players can refer to these drills to strengthen fundamental strokes.

"Advanced and Tournament-Level Drills" are planned for those who value winning or have championship aspirations. This section emphasizes greater control by having the player stroke to smaller targets, using a wide variety of drills. Development of the all-court game and controlled power are accented. Many champions have employed these drills.

The major advantages of drilling are:

1. Many more balls are hit in drilling than in regular play, thus shot mastery takes place more rapidly.
2. Specific weaknesses can be focused upon and remedied.
3. This drilling technique is not as competitive as playing matches, so the player sometimes finds it more enjoyable.
4. The drills and exercises are excellent motivators since they offer constant challenge.
5. The possibility of becoming "over-tennised" through too much competitive play is minimized.

6. Unlike the playing of games, drilling allows players of different skill levels to play together while deriving mutual benefit.

7. When there is a shortage of courts, drilling enables six to eight players to develop their strokes on a single court.

8. Drilling gives the player an excellent appraisal of the effectiveness of individual shots. He would learn, for example, that his overhead smash is more precise to one corner than to another, and his forehand dropshot is weaker than his backhand. Therefore, he would know which high-percentage shots should be used on crucial points.

TENNIS DRILLS

SECTION I

DRILLING BASICS

Carefully concentrate when you drill and practice. Pretend every ball has the importance of a match point. Do not practice one way and play sets another, since it limits tennis improvement.

Use lively balls. Have ten to twenty lively balls when you go on the court. Dead balls stay on your racket too long, and give you delusions of grandeur about control. If a ball has been out of the can more than two or three months and can be pushed in more than one-quarter of an inch, it is probably dead. When dropped from your eye level, in moderate temperature, the ball should rebound to about your waist level. You may use pressureless balls for drilling since they do not lose their liveliness. Keep dead balls for hard-hitting drills on the backboard.

Get to the ball quickly. Get to the ball as quickly as you can so that you will be able to stroke unhurriedly. By being relatively still when you contact the ball, greater accuracy is possible. Watch the ball go to and from your drilling partner's racket in order to determine, at the earliest possible moment, the direction of his shot.

As your partner is about to strike the ball, have your knees slightly bent, and bounce on the balls of your feet. This "ready hop" improves your chances of getting to the ball fast. Hustle at full speed for every ball, even when your partner hits it ten feet out of court. The balls you are forced to take on the run are especially valuable. Take the ball on the first bounce only, or volley it; do not allow it to hit the ground twice. Take your racket back fast while you are approaching the ball.

Stroke the ball early. On groundstrokes, take the ball just before it reaches its peak, or at waist height. Do not take too much time to stroke the ball after it bounces. By standing on or near the baseline, you will be forced to take balls early that land deep in your court. Stroking early helps keep your partner on the defensive. In doing this, your partner is allowed less time to retrieve your shot, and your hitting angle improves.

Increase pace. Say to yourself, "I am going to hit ten percent harder in the drills today than I did yesterday." Increase pace by relaxing the arm, especially on the backswing; moving body weight forward helps. At advanced stages, leg power can be applied as well as going off the ground to stroke the ball. Make sure that before the start of the forward swing of a ground stroke your racket is pointed to the back fence in order to allow a half circle, or 180° swing.

Do not overhit. If your balls miss the court boundaries by more than five or six feet, or if they land in the middle or the bottom of the net, you are probably swinging faster than you should. However, it is important to find out what your limit of controlled speed is. Bad errors can often be avoided by watching the ball carefully as it comes across the net and meets your racket.

HOW OFTEN SHOULD YOU PRACTICE?

The more balls that you stroke, the stronger you will become as a player. Ball control comes from hitting a lot of balls. If Jones hits 5,000 balls in his lifetime, and Smith 10,000, providing other abilities are equal, Smith will beat Jones. Playing four times a week is better than twice, and two sessions a day are better than one.

There is no substitute for ball control and deeply grooved or "overlearned" strokes that are achieved through diligent effort. No outstanding player has spent less than seven to ten years (320 to 350 days a year) in intensive and serious practice. During your early tennis years you should plan on drilling fifty to sixty percent of the total time you play the game.

WHERE AND WITH WHOM SHOULD YOU SCHEDULE PRACTICE?

In the advanced stage of development, play matches in a variety of settings, against a variety of opponents, using a variety of makes of balls. This will lead to competitive maturity, and will enable you to quickly adjust to vastly differing tournament conditions.

Meet tough competition most of the time. In addition to playing superior players, occasionally play some who are inferior, since against them you can develop non-percentage shots and strategies. Be sure not to sacrifice form for the sake of winning.

SECRET OF TENNIS IMPROVEMENT IN ONE SENTENCE

The combination of a large number of balls, hit with correct grips and strokes in a controlled and powerful manner, toward mental targets requiring adjustment, and against tough competition, is what brings about tennis improvement.

DRILLS FOR BEGINNERS

Drill 1

PREPARATION EXERCISES FOR TENNIS

The better you can throw and catch a ball and coordinate body movements, the more rapid your tennis progress will be. Show me a slow learner in tennis and I will show you one with very limited experience in ball games. Running, jumping, and dodging, preferably with a ball, are excellent for tennis preparation. A child can start developing ball skills as early as two years old.

BALL THROWING AND CATCHING

Throwing hard means serving hard. Almost every top player able to hit a powerful serve or overhead smash is capable of throwing a ball fast and far. In order to have a "big" (i.e., hard) serve, you should be able to throw a tennis ball from the baseline of the court, across the net, hitting the opposite tennis court fence, without a bounce. If you have high aspirations, you should learn to throw and throw hard. It is important that you throw with the same arm that you plan to use for serving and playing tennis.

Cock the wrist and throw overhand. Swing the arm back, and cock the wrist just before you bring the arm forward (Fig. 1.1A). This cocked or laid-back position of the wrist is almost identical with the racket drop on the serve and smash (Fig. 1.1B). Throw with an overhand motion directly above your shoulder; do not

Fig. 1.1 Learn to use the wrist to throw and eventually to serve.

1.1A Correct wrist position before throwing or serving.

1.1B Laying back the wrist when serving is similar to cocking the wrist before throwing.

sidearm the pitch. As the arm goes forward, the upper arm should pass close to the ear (Figs. 1.2A and B).

Practice catching a ball. Catching the ball develops hand–eye coordination. This will teach you balance, transference of weight, and develop the hand and wrist. Practice catching with the hand you will be using to hold the racket, as well as with both hands.

Fig. 1.2   Correct overhead throwing motion for tennis.

1.2A   Cock the wrist.

1.2B   Release the ball directly overhead.

JUMPING ROPE

This improves footwork and condition, and is especially helpful for the beginner who has not been athletically active. Some professional tennis players jump rope. Try jumping, using only the left foot (15 times), and then the right foot (15 times). If you can jump three hundred times without stopping, using both feet, you are in excellent shape. Even if a park is unavailable for running, you can attain good physical condition by jumping rope in your backyard or hallway (preferably on a soft surface).

Fig. 1.3   Practice jumping rope.

TABLE TENNIS

Table tennis teaches ball timing and footwork. You become familiar with ball spins caused by forehand and backhand slices and drives.

Fig. 1.4   Table tennis teaches hand-eye coordination.

Drill 2
GRIPS: BECOMING FAMILIAR WITH THEM

You have a choice of how you wish to hold (grip) your racket. These choices are:

1. You can use an Eastern forehand grip (Fig. 2.1) and change the hand position for the backhand grip (Figs. 2.2A and B). The Eastern forehand grip has power potential since the arm and hand are completely behind the stroke; or,

Fig.   2.1   Eastern forehand grip—used for forehand groundstroke.

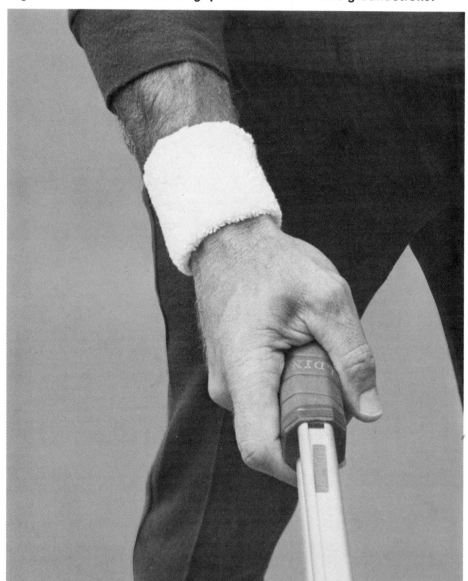

2. You can use one grip for all shots by using either the Continental grip (identical to backhand grip in Fig. 2.2) or the Australian grip (Fig. 2.3). Using either grip saves time and effort since you do not have to make a change; or,

Fig. 2.2 Backhand or Continental grip—used for backhand groundstroke, serving, volleying and smashing.

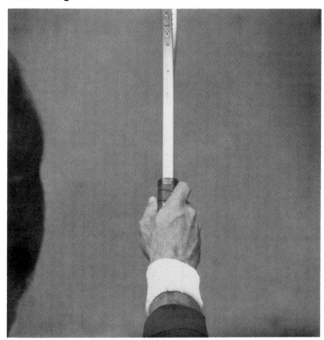

2.2A   Top view.

Fig. 2.3   Australian grip—used for all strokes.

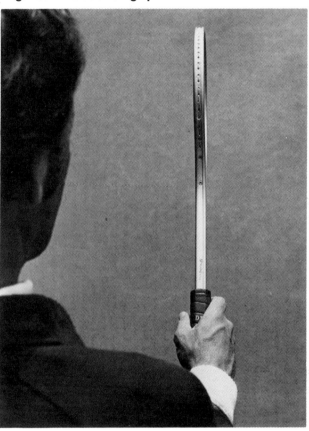

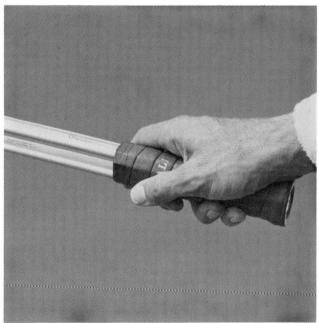

2.2B   Side view.

3. You can use a two-handed backhand (Fig. 2.4), a two-handed forehand, or use two-handed grips on forehand and backhand. Two-handed grips produce overspin power, and offer disguise in shot placement.

Fig. 2.4 Two-handed backhand grip. You may use an Eastern forehand grip with your right hand when using two hands for the backhand.

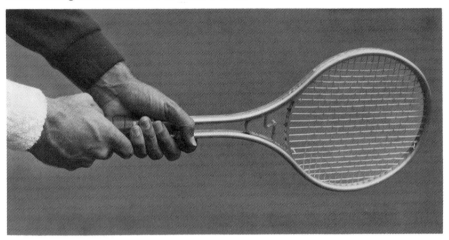

SPIN THE RACKET TO OVERLEARN
THE PROPER GRIP

After learning to hold your racket properly, close your eyes and spin the racket in your hand to locate the correct grip (Fig. 2.5). You will soon recognize "feel spots." For example, you will discover that a certain joint of a finger should rest on a particular place of the handle. Overlearning the proper grip helps to prevent losing feel of the racket ("choking") when you reach the playing stage.

Fig. 2.5 Spinning the racket to become familiar with the grip.

Drill **3**

ISOMETRICS TO STRENGTHEN HAND, WRIST, AND FOREARM

You need strength to hold the racket firmly as it strikes a ball coming toward you with great speed. To gain strength, it is advisable to perform isometrics. (Figs. 3.1 and 3.2). Press the racket against the wall as hard as possible for fifteen seconds, rest a few seconds, and repeat for another fifteen seconds. Do the exercise on the forehand and backhand sides, using the correct grips.

Fig. 3.1   Using isometrics to strengthen forehand muscles.

Fig. 3.2   Strengthening backhand muscles.

Drill **4**

BALL DRIBBLING USING FOREHAND

This exercise introduces the ball to your racket strings. As you dribble (bouncing the ball to the ground with the racket), make sure you are using the proper forehand grip. Make contact with the ball at waist level. First, do the exercise in a stationary position, trying not to move either foot (Fig. 4.1). Count the number you can do in a minute. As you get better, try dribbling as you run.

Fig. 4.1   Ball dribbling, using forehand.

Drill **5**

BALL BUMPING-UP AND LEARNING THE SWEET SPOT

BALL BUMPING-UP ON FOREHAND

Using the forehand grip, bump the ball up in the air without allowing it to fall to the ground (Fig. 5.1).

Fig. 5.1   Ball bumping-up on forehand.

BALL BUMPING-UP ON BACKHAND

Using the backhand grip, bump the ball up in the air as many times as you can without letting the ball fall to the ground. Make sure your knuckles are facing the sky, and your palm is facing the ground when holding the racket (Fig. 5.2).

When you can bump up twenty consecutive balls on the forehand and backhand, without moving your feet, you will be ready to learn the forehand and backhand drives.

Fig. 5.2   Ball bumping-up on backhand.

LEARNING THE SWEET SPOT

As you bump the ball up in the air on the forehand side, you will find out which part of the racket face (strings) sends the ball off with the most power and firmness. You will soon discover that the center of the racket strings ("sweet spot") is the most desirable place to contact the ball. Solid hits also occur outside of the sweet spot though maximum power (leverage) will be lacking (Fig. 5.3).

Fig. 5.3   Learning the sweet spot. Solid hits can also occur in the gray area around and below the sweet spot.

Sweet Spot

Drill **6**

BALL PICKUP TECHNIQUES

Practicing ball pickup techniques gives you additional ball contact with the racket. By not bending over to pick up a ball you are saved energy, and back strain is minimized. Though you may exert considerable effort in learning ball pickups, the dividend received after mastery will be a smooth, natural, and effortless technique. For those who wish to appear experienced, fluid ball pickup skills are an asset (Figs. 6.1A–C; 6.2A–C; 6.3A–C).

Fig. 6.1   Ball pickup technique 1: Ball scooping-up method.

6.1A Pull the ball toward you rapidly on the ground.

6.1B Wait for moving ball to come to racket.

6.1C Ball is scooped up and flipped to left hand. (This ball pickup method should not be used on a hard-surface court since racket head damage might occur.)

Fig. 6.2 Ball pickup technique 2: Advanced method.

6.2A Ready to tap stationary ball with racket.

6.2B Three quick taps are usually needed to pick up the ball. (Make the first tap very firm.)

6.2C On the third tap, the ball rebounds high from the ground and is caught with the left hand. Using a choked-up racket grip (hand above leather) will make this difficult technique slightly easier. Picking up a ball using the advanced method is also a means of testing to learn if a racket is playable; a dead racket will not pick up a ball in this manner.

Fig. 6.3 Ball pickup technique 3: Lifting-foot method.

6.3A Press stationary ball against foot with the racket.

6.3B Lift the foot ten or twelve inches from the ground as racket is holding the ball against the foot.

6.3C Ball is released by foot, bounces to ground, and is scooped up with the racket and flipped to the left hand.

Drill 7

WALL-TO-WALL SWINGING FOR GROUNDSTROKE DEVELOPMENT

Now that you have developed racket and ball feel skills, you are ready to learn the basic strokes. Starting with your back to the wall, make a forehand ground-stroke (without a ball), by swinging from low to high, touching the wall at the beginning and end of the stroke (Figs. 7.1A and B). Repeat the exercise using the backhand (Figs. 7.2A and B).

Fig. 7.1   Learning the forehand drive by swinging wall to wall and low to high.

7.1A   Start with racket extended behind, and against the wall. Weight should be on the back foot.

7.1B   Finish with racket high and against the wall. At the completion of the stroke the weight should be on the forward foot.

You will learn the desirable length (180° or a half circle) of the normal stroke. This drill reinforces the low-to-high direction of the swing that produces top spin and safety on shots. In addition, you practice weight transference as you must shift weight from the back foot to the front to execute this exercise properly. Swinging wall to wall has the advantage of preventing the elbow from leading in making a backhand drive.

Fig. 7.2 Learning the backhand drive by swinging wall to wall and low to high.

7.2A   Start with racket extended low and against the wall.

7.2B   Finish with racket high and against the wall.

Drill **8**

EXERCISES FOR SHOULDER TURN, RHYTHM, AND WEIGHT TRANSFERENCE

DOING THE SHOULDER TURN

The shoulder turn is an essential source of stroke power. A method of acquiring this is shown in the accompanying illustrations (Figs. 8.1A and B).

Standing with hands on hips facing sideline, do a shoulder turn until both shoulders are parallel with, and you are facing, the net. The heel of your back foot will automatically leave the ground.

Fig. 8.1 Practicing the forehand shoulder turn without racket.

8.1A   Hands on hips with side to net.

8.1B   Turn shoulders to net (rear heel automatically comes off ground.)

Repeat this exercise using a racket (Figs. 8.2A and B). Practice this shoulder turn on both backhand and forehand sides. Facing the opposite sideline would be the start of the backhand shoulder turn.

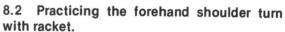

8.2 Practicing the forehand shoulder turn with racket.

8.2A   Ready to swing.

8.2B   Swing.

SWINGING FOR RHYTHM

Developing a stroking rhythm is desirable for stroke uniformity and good ball timing. These exercises (Figs. 8.3A–C, and 8.4A–C) can be done as easily in the living room of an apartment as on a tennis court. The transference of weight from back to front foot should occur in exercises 8.1, 8.2, 8.3, and 8.4.

Fig. 8.3   Swinging for rhythm on the forehand drive using a straight backswing.

8.3A   Back and . . . (this is the backswing).

8.3B   Forward and . . . (this is the forward swing).

8.3C   Back and . . .

Fig. 8.4   Swinging for rhythm on the backhand drive using a straight backswing.

8.4A   Back and . . .

8.4B   Forward and . . .

8.4C   Back and . . .

Drill 9

GROUNDSTROKE DRIVE DEVELOPMENT

TURN, STEP, AND SWING

Develop your groundstrokes, *without* a ball, in the following manner (Figs. 9.1A–E, and 9.2A–E):

1. Stand in the ready position.
2. Turn sideways and take your racket back.
3. Step with the proper foot in the direction you are planning to stroke the ball.
4. Swing your racket from low to high.
5. Hold the follow-through.

As you are doing this exercise say to yourself, "Ready, turn, step, swing, hold." Do this many times on the forehand side, grooving the proper form, then switch and work on the backhand. Alternate from forehand, to backhand, to forehand, etc.

If you are using an Eastern forehand grip, make sure you change for the backhand. Those electing the single grip method, Australian or Continental, do not have to change. If you are unsure of this, refer to Drill 2.

While in the ready position, grip with your free hand just above the other hand holding the racket. By placing your left hand an inch or two above your right one, you will be able to get the racket back faster, and you will be more relaxed than waiting with a hand up on the racket throat.

Fig. 9.1 Practice the forehand drive and hold the follow-through.

9.1A Ready. (Keep hands close together on the racket.)

9.1B Turn shoulders, and bring racket back. Weight is on the right foot.

9.1C   Step toward target with left foot.

9.1E   Hold follow-through for a couple of seconds.

9.1D   Swing. (Weight shifts to front foot.)

Fig. 9.2 Practice the backhand drive and hold the follow-through.

9.2A   Ready.

9.2C   Step toward target with right foot.

9.2B   Turn shoulders and bring racket back.

9.2D   Swing.

9.2E   Hold follow-through for a couple of seconds.

TO INSURE CORRECT RACKET POSITION

Place a coin on the edge of the racket throat. Swing *very* slowly forward and keep the coin on the racket throughout the swing (Fig. 9.3). This exercise prevents your racket head from turning over, and keeps the racket face perpendicular to the ground. Mishit balls are minimized when the racket head stays perpendicular to the ground during a stroke.

Fig. 9.3   Place coin on racket throat to insure the racket face stays perpendicular (on edge) to ground throughout entire forehand drive stroke.

ADVANTAGE OF STROKING WITHOUT A BALL

Executing the proper stroke without a ball is an excellent method of learning. When a ball is introduced many beginners use poor form and forget the proper technique. If you repeatedly practice the correct form without a ball, you will continue to use that same form when you begin to stroke with a ball. After overlearning the correct stroke, it becomes difficult to perform improperly. Periodic professional lessons in the early stages of learning are especially valuable.

WHAT IS A DESIRABLE STROKE?

Make sure you are developing strokes within the range of correctness. *A desirable stroke is executed with minimum effort to achieve the maximum in control and power.* Good strokes are based upon efficiency (good form) and simplicity (no unnecessary motion).

Drill **10**

KEEP RACKET STRINGS ON THE BALL

To gain control and power in stroking, keep the strings on the ball as long as possible after contact. You can do this by bending the knees, transferring weight from the back to front foot, and by pressing the strings of the racket against the ball in the direction you are hitting.

One method of practicing this is to hold the racket above, and stroke over, a row of seven balls (Fig. 10.1). Pretend you are making contact with the first ball, and slowly swing the racket head over each successive ball until you have passed over the seventh. These seven balls represent the approximate distance you can keep the ball on the racket. Use some low-to-high racket direction as you practice. Try the forehand as well as the backhand drive.

Fig. 10.1 Guide the racket above a row of seven balls to learn to keep racket strings on the ball.

HITTING THROUGH THE BALL

Another way you can simulate "hitting through" a ball is to use the net as a guide (Fig. 10.2). Stand facing the net and extend your racket head until it touches the net. Guide the racket head along the top or middle of the net until you can no longer make contact. Then simulate a full groundstroke guiding your racket along the net as you would a ball. When your racket can no longer touch the net, you will discover how long your racket strings can stay on the ball in actual play. In this exercise you are pretending to hit a ball toward the sideline and parallel with the net. A wall or fence can also be used.

When contacting a ball with a groundstroke, volley, or overhead, picture your strings firmly pressing against the ball rather than quickly hitting it. Think of yourself as guiding or conveying the ball in the direction you want.

Fig. 10.2   Guide racket along net to acquire the feel of keeping racket strings on ball.

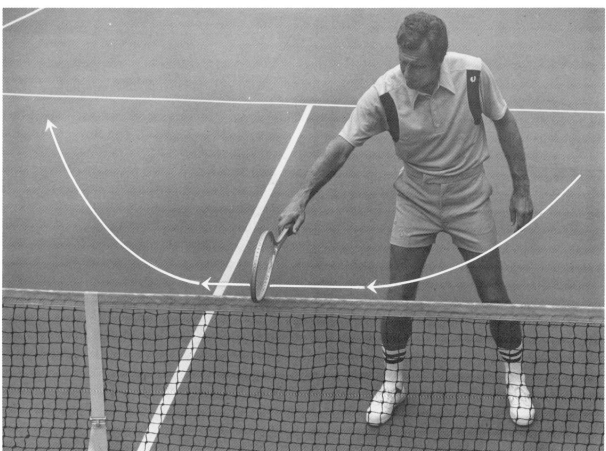

Drill **11**

GROUNDSTROKE DRIVES FROM A SELF-DROPPED BALL

BOUNCE AND STROKE BALL TO FENCE

The first step in learning to stroke with a ball is to take the racket back on the forehand, slowly drop the ball about two or three feet away from you, and stroke the ball to the fence or wall. (Figs. 11.1A–C). After you can hit the fence fifteen consecutive times, start working on the backhand (Figs. 11.2A and B).

Fig. 11.1   Bouncing a ball and stroking a forehand drive to a fence.

11.1A   Ready to drop ball on ground. (Racket head is perpendicular to ground, weight is on back foot, and point of ball contact will be opposite front foot.)

11.1B   Swing. (Shift weight from back to front foot and keep racket head perpendicular to ground.)

11.1C   Hold the follow-through.

Fig. 11.2   Bouncing a ball and stroking a backhand drive to a fence.

11.2A   Ready to bounce ball and swing. (Racket head is perpendicular to ground, weight is on back foot, and point of ball contact will be slightly forward of front foot.)

11.2B   Hold the follow-through. (Shift weight from back to front foot and keep racket head perpendicular to ground.)

BOUNCE AND STROKE BALL ON COURT

Mentally mark the four sections of a court (one to four), and bounce and stroke the ball to each of the areas with the forehand and then the backhand drive (Fig. 11.3). Stand just behind the service line on the opposite side of the net of the four targets.

Fig. 11.3 Bouncing a ball and stroking a backhand drive toward a numbered part of the court.

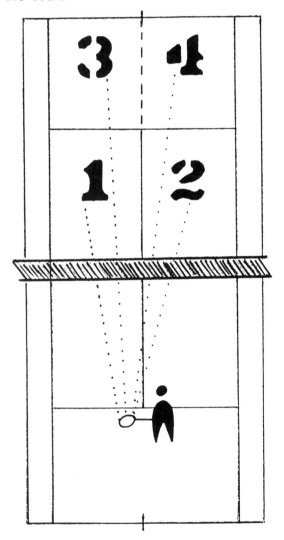

Drill 12

GROUNDSTROKE DRIVES WITH SHORT SWING

Occasionally you must hit a ball by taking the racket back a shorter distance before swinging. For example, a short swing is used when returning a fast service, or in half volleying. In this drill, you learn to use a short backswing with an abbreviated forward swing.

Hold the racket one foot behind the point where you are contacting the ball, then drop the ball and stroke it to the fence or wall. Once the racket is in place, only swing forward; do not bring the racket back any further. A partner can place his racket behind yours to make sure you do not extend the backswing (Figs. 12.1A and B, and 12.2A and B).

Fig. 12.1 Forehand drive with short swing using partner as a brace to prevent backswing.

12.1A   Ready to bounce ball and swing.

12.1B   Hold the follow-through.

Fig. 12.2   Backhand drive with short swing using partner as a brace to prevent backswing.

12.2A   Ready to bounce ball and swing.

12.2B   Hold the follow-through.

Drill **13**

GROUNDSTROKE DRIVES FROM A TOSSED BALL— STATIONARY POSITION

In this drill, stand with your racket fully back on the forehand side, while a partner slowly tosses you the ball underhand from twenty feet away. After the ball bounces, slowly stroke the ball to your partner. Do not move your feet, only transfer weight from back to front foot. Hold the follow-through for a couple of seconds (Figs. 13A and B). A *very* slow and accurate toss is essential. After gaining accuracy on the forehand, start stroking with the backhand.

Try to catch the ball. The tosser should catch the stroked ball on the fly (before it bounces), even leaping if necessary. For some beginners, coordinating the hands and eyes in catching is almost as valuable a drill as stroking the ball.

Fig. 13   Forehand drive from a tossed ball—stationary position.

13A   Ready to receive tossed ball. X is where tossed ball should bounce, which is halfway between the tosser and the place where the racket contacts the ball. (Tossed ball should be aimed about 3 feet to the right of the hitter.)

13B Hold the follow-through after the swing while tosser catches ball. Raised heel indicates proper transfer of weight.

Drill 14

FOOTWORK DRILLS COMBINED WITH GROUNDSTROKES— WITHOUT BALL

SHUFFLE STEP FOR NEAR BALLS

It is desirable for the beginning player to practice footwork drills so court movement will become smooth and quick. For balls from six to ten feet away, shuffle step to the ball, then turn, step, and swing (Figs. 14.1A–E, and 14.2A–E). When shuffling to your right, be sure to pick up your right foot and move it to your right. When shuffling to your left, be sure to step out with your left foot first. Do not cross one leg over another.

Fig. 14.1   Shuffle step and then a forehand drive.

14.1A   Ready.

14.1B   Step with right foot.

14.1C Together (bring left foot next to right foot).

14.1E Step and swing (step with left foot toward target and swing forehand drive).

14.1D Step, turn shoulders, with right foot pointing toward sideline, and bring racket back.

Fig. 14.2   Shuffle step and then a backhand drive.

14.2A   Ready.

14.2B   Step with left foot.

14.2C   Together (bring right foot next to left foot).

14.2D   Step, turn shoulders, with left foot pointing toward sideline, and bring racket back.

14.2E   Step and swing (step with right foot toward target and swing backhand drive).

RUN FOR DISTANT BALLS

When going for balls more than ten feet away, it is best to run. Call this a crossover step (Fig. 14.3). When approaching the ball, it is best to shorten your steps.

Fig. 14.3   Crossover step (running) toward a ball on backhand side. Take racket back immediately as you run to meet the ball so that your stroke will not be rushed.

FOOTWORK FOR BALLS HIT AT YOU

When a ball is hit directly at you, it is desirable to use the footwork recommended in Figs. 14.4A–C. When you have a choice between forehand or backhand, naturally, use your most reliable stroke.

A note of encouragement: although the foot drills might seem a little difficult at this point, you will be pleasantly surprised at how quickly they become natural for you.

Fig. 14.4   Moving out of the way of a ball coming directly at you and stroking a forehand drive.

14.4A   Ready.

14.4B   Turn shoulders, bring racket back, and step with right foot behind body.

14.4C   Step and swing (step with left foot toward target, and swing forehand drive).

GROUNDSTROKE DRIVES FROM A TOSSED BALL— AS YOU MOVE

Once you can accurately hit forehand and backhand drives from a stationary position, begin stroking the ball while moving. Your partner stands with his back to the fence and from ten or fifteen feet away slowly tosses the ball underhand to your backhand. After the ball bounces once, stroke the ball back to the tosser who catches it on the fly (Figs. 15A and B).

Use any step you wish to get to the ball. Take the racket back quickly so that the stroke will not be rushed. Practice forehands as well as backhands.

Fig. 15   Stroking a backhand drive while moving.

15A   Tosser is about to release the ball with gentle, underhand pitch. Move rapidly to meet the ball.

15B   Stroke ball to tosser with backhand drive.

Drill 16

GROUNDSTROKE DRIVE RALLYING ON BACKBOARD

AIM FOR TARGET—TAKE BALL ON FIRST BOUNCE

For a beginner, the backboard is excellent for developing strokes. Paint, crayon, or chalk a net line and a target so you will always be aiming for a specific area. Start rallying about eight or ten feet from the wall, and as you gain control and pace, gradually move to a distance of twenty to twenty-five feet from the target (Fig. 16.1). Do not allow the ball to bounce twice while rallying on a wall, or on a court. Practice forehand drives, backhand drives, and then combine them. Count the number of your consecutive good shots.

HIT WHILE MOVING AND CHANGE PACE

After becoming proficient, make an additional target so that angles will be wider, forcing you to hit on the move. Hit four or five shots at normal pace, and then blast the ball. If you have difficulty handling a normal ball, use a slightly dead or punctured ball that will allow for better control and additional time for stroke preparation.

Fig. 16.1 Groundstroke drive rallying on backboard.

If a large backboard area is unavailable, you can develop control by hitting against a cellar wall or hallway (Fig. 16.2). To avoid defacing property, use a small piece of removable tape as your target and stand six or seven feet away as you maintain a soft rally.

Fig. 16.2   Developing "feel" on groundstrokes, using short backswing, in an area of limited space.

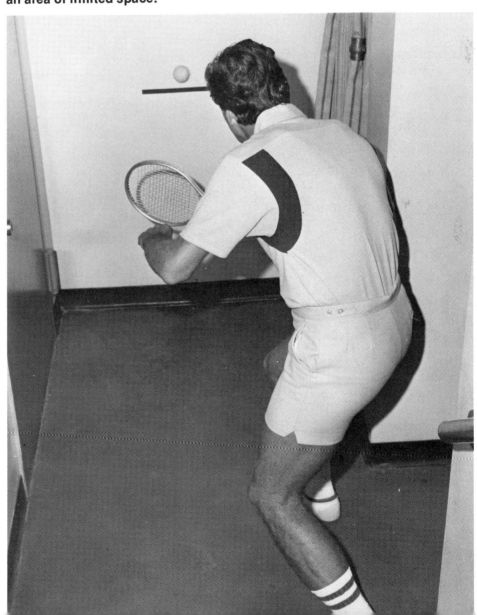

Drill 17

TETHERED BALL
PRACTICE

If a backboard or tennis court is unavailable, practicing with a tethered ball can temporarily suffice. A tethered ball is fastened to a part nylon, part rubber cord that is attached to a metal base (Fig. 17.1). This device automatically returns the ball to an area near you after it is stroked.

The tethered ball can be used in any open flat area; it develops ball control and hand–wrist strength. Be sure to use proper form while doing this; do not take wild "swipes" at the ball (Fig. 17.2).

Fig. 17.1 Practicing with a tethered ball device. This ball trainer has a heavy base with a ball attached by a long elastic cord.

Fig. 17.2 Stroking position when one person uses tethered ball device.

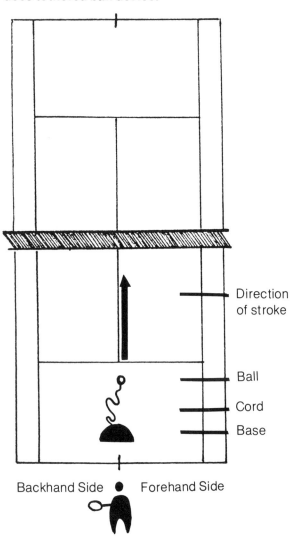

Direction of stroke

Ball

Cord

Base

Backhand Side   Forehand Side

Drill **18**

SHORT-DISTANCE RALLYING

SERVICE-BOX RALLYING

Begin rallying with a partner in a small area. Control and feel for the ball are then developed. You will learn to stroke slowly using a short backswing. Five exercises are listed (Fig. 18.1) and should be practiced in the correct sequence from A through E. You have mastered each drill when you average eight or ten balls in a rally.

Fig. 18.1   Service-box rallying

A.   Rally from box 2 to 4 using forehands only.

B.   Rally from box 2 to 4 using backhands only.

C.   Rally from box 2 to 3 using forehands only.

D.   Rally from box 1 to 4 using backhands only.

E.   Rally from box 2 to 4 using forehands and backhands.

SERVICE-BOX GAME

Play a ten-point game in the same manner as Exercise 18.1E. Standing behind your service box, bounce the ball and stroke it to your partner's service box. Whoever wishes may put the ball in play for the first and succeeding points. Take all balls after the first bounce. Both forehands and backhands may be used (Fig. 18.2).

A player wins the point if his partner hits a ball outside of the proper service box or into the net so that a rally is broken. If a player fails to put the ball in play correctly, he also loses the point. The game ends and a new one begins when a player has ten points. To win the game, you must be at least two points ahead of your partner, thus there may be games ending at 12–10, 15–13, etc.

Fig. 18.2 Service-box game.

PAVEMENT OR DRIVEWAY RALLYING

If a tennis court is unavailable, short-distance rallying can be done in a driveway or on some kind of pavement. Tie string or rope to two posts, garbage cans, or trees. Place newspapers, towels, or sheets over the cord and begin rallying (Fig. 18.3).

Fig. 18.3 If a court is unavailable, you can develop ball control skills in other areas.

Drill **19**

BASELINE RALLYING

In this drill, you will use forehand and backhand drives from farther back in the court than the service box. Stand just inside the baseline, and start a rally by dropping the ball on the ground, and slowly stroke it to your partner who is on the opposite baseline. Hit all balls after the first bounce and aim toward your partner (Fig. 19). To avoid spending excessive time retrieving balls, and to allow more hitting time, take a large number of lively balls to the court.

As you and your partner become skillful, move two or three yards behind the baseline. Use this as your backcourt home base, returning to it after each shot. In order to attain depth of shot, aim your slow drives five or six feet above the net.

Fig. 19 Deep-court rallying.

Drill

SERVICE: RACKET TOSS

An effective method of associating serving with throwing is to take a broken racket and throw it for distance from the baseline of a tennis court across the net (Fig. 20). This will indicate service power potential. Do it a number of times and compare the distance you can throw with others. If an adult player can toss the racket from his baseline, across the net, beyond the opposite baseline, he has potential for developing a ''big'' service.

Fig. 20   Throwing an old racket for distance to discover service power potential.

SERVICE: LEARNING
THE ACTION

You will now learn the fundamental action. Do not toss or hit any balls in this exercise. Use either the Continental or forehand grip, preferably the Continental. Tournament players use the Continental grip for service since spin and variety are easily achieved. (Figs. 2.1 and 2.2 on pages 10 and 11 illustrate these grips.) Before learning the specific steps of serving, keep the following principles in mind:

Racket drop is important. Although differing somewhat in style, all good serves have one element in common. This is the racket drop or back-scratching motion which starts the forward swing (Fig. 21.1).

Swing directly overhead. Make sure that on your forward swing the racket is extended directly overhead, and the upper arm passes close to the ear (Fig. 21.2). Do not serve sidearm.

Three serving actions are detailed below. You can select the action that is most suitable for your experience and ability. Practice the service action many times without the ball.

Fig. 21.1 Racket drop or back-scratching motion. As the distance from the racket to the player's back increases, so does the power potential. Racket points straight down to ground just before forward swing is made.

Fig. 21.2   When serving, swing extended racket directly overhead.

SIMPLE SERVICE

A simple service, excellent for beginners, starts with the racket straight above the shoulder (Figs. 21.3A–E). It has three components: the ball is tossed in the air, the racket is dropped behind the back, and the swing at the ball is made.

Fig. 21.3 Simple service.

21.3A   Ready to serve. Feet are 12–18 inches apart, and front toe rests one inch behind baseline.

21.3B   Toss (slowly).

21.3C   Drop racket head behind back so that it points straight down to ground.

21.3E   Follow through so that racket points to fence behind player.

21.3D Swing (by reaching high and directly overhead).

CLASSIC SERVICE

The classic or advanced service action begins with the racket pointing toward the service box where you are aiming (Figs. 21.4A–F). It is easiest learned from the ready position (Fig. 21.4A) by taking the racket and ball down together (Fig. 21.4B), and then bringing them up together as the ball is tossed (Fig. 21.4C). The racket head is then dropped (Fig. 21.4D), and the swing is made (Fig. 21.4E). Be sure to follow through (Fig. 21.4F).

Fig. 21.4   Classic or advanced service.

21.4A   Ready to serve.

21.4B   Arms down together.

21.4C   Arms up together.

21.4E   Swing (wrist snaps and player thinks of accelerating *after* ball contact is made).

21.4D   Drop racket head.

21.4F   Follow-through.

ABBREVIATED SERVICE

The abbreviated or energy-saving service (Figs. 21.5A-E) is similar to the classic service, except the down-together motion of the arms is eliminated. You point the racket where you are aiming the serve (Fig. 21.5A), and simply bring the arms up together as you toss the ball (Fig. 21.5B) and then drop the racket head (Fig. 21.5C). You then swing and follow through (Figs. 21.5D and E).

Practice swinging your racket as hard as possible in order to develop speed on service (Fig. 21.6). Make sure that you use proper form when serving for speed. Beginning players cannot use great racket-head speed on any shot since it will result in too many errors. As you gain in ability, increase racket-head speed.

Fig. 21.5   Abbreviated service.

21.5B   Arms up together.

21.5A   Ready to serve.

21.5C   Drop racket head.

21.5D   Swing.

21.5E   Follow-through.

Fig. 21.6   Swinging for speed on service. Try to swing hard enough to hear the "whoosh" as the wind goes through the strings.

Drill **22**

SERVICE: BALL TOSS

An accurate ball toss is essential if a service is to have maximum control and power.

HEIGHT OF TOSS

First you will locate the proper height of your ball toss. Grasp the ball with the last joint of your fingers and thumb (Fig. 22.1). Hold your racket as high as you can reach, straight up in the air and above your shoulder. Toss the ball about a foot higher than the top of your extended racket (Fig. 22.2). (Release the ball as late as possible, or at about eye level, to help guarantee a precise toss.) Toss the ball up very slowly. Try a dozen of these height-finding tosses.

Fig. 22.1 Service toss should be made from last joint of fingers and thumb.

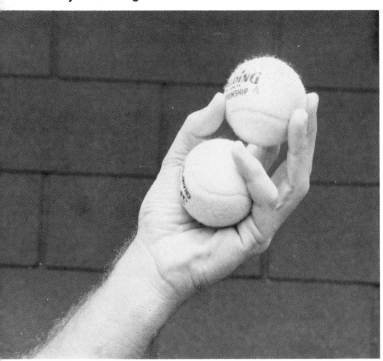

Fig. 22.2 Height-finding toss for service. Target is one foot above extended racket.

TOSS STRAIGHT UP

To insure that your toss goes straight up, practice tossing a ball adjacent to, and parallel with, a fence post. With your racket extended above your shoulder, toss the ball the same height you learned in the previous exercise. Minimize the amount of right–left movement, or drift of the ball. An incorrect toss is easily seen since the ball is silhouetted clearly against the fence (Fig. 22.3). Try ten or twelve tosses.

TOSS WITH BACKSWING

After selecting your service action from Drill 21 or an instructor, coordinate the ball toss with the first part of the racket backswing. In the simple service, as illustrated in Fig. 21.3, when the racket is extended directly above the shoulder the toss is made. The racket head is then dropped behind the back. In the classic (Fig. 21.4) and abbreviated (Fig. 21.5) service actions, the toss occurs in the up-together movement of the arms. Do fifteen ball tosses, allowing the ball to fall to the ground.

Fig. 22.3 Practice service ball toss, using fence post as guide, to minimize ball drift. The toss should go straight up and should drift very little from right to left.

PLACING TOSS IN TARGET ON GROUND

Do the entire service racket backswing, placing your racket in the back-scratching position, and practice tossing the ball in the air and having it land on a target on the ground (Fig. 22.4). In the simple service, toss the ball and drop the racket behind the back. If you have a classic motion, practice the down-together of the arms, up-together with the ball toss, and then drop the racket to the back-scratching position. If you use the abbreviated swing, go up together with both arms as the toss is made, and then drop your racket behind your back. Try thirty or more of these tosses without swinging at the ball.

Fig. 22.4   Tossing service ball and attempting to drop it on racket cover used as target. Beginner's toss should land in front and slightly to the right of server.

CATCHING THE SERVICE TOSS

Finally, instead of allowing the tossed ball to hit the ground, catch it with a straight tossing arm (Fig. 22.5). The ball should be caught above and in front of your head. Catching a tossed ball in this manner develops a late ball release, and helps train the eye to stay upward when the racket contacts the ball.

Fig. 22.5 Catching service ball toss with a straight arm.

Drill **23**

SERVICE PRACTICE

COORDINATING RACKET ACTION WITH TOSS

After learning a service motion and an accurate ball toss, practice serving a ball against a wall or fence. On the first few serves, toss the ball higher than usual so you will have more time to attain the racket drop (Fig. 23.1). The proper back-scratching action is the key item at this stage of service development. After you can hit the wall with fifteen consecutive balls from a twenty-five foot distance, you can move to the court and practice normal serving.

In competition, a player is allowed two serves. If the first serve does not land within the correct service box, you are allowed a second try. The first service should be as powerful a stroke as possible.

Fig. 23.1 Practice serving to a fence until you can coordinate your toss with your racket swing.

DEVELOPING THE SECOND SERVICE

It is very important when you miss your first service that you have a dependable second serve since this is your final opportunity to get the ball in play without penalty. Do not think of power until you can serve several consecutive balls in the proper service box with a good racket drop. In other words, develop a reliable second service before you attempt power and placement near corners, as you would on a first service. Standing near the center mark, practice serving to the left and right courts.

BEGINNER'S UNDERHAND SERVICE

If you have to play a game, but are unable to serve overhand with accuracy, simply serve underhand slowly and with a high (safe) trajectory (Figs. 23.2A and B). Toss the ball only a foot above your waist, and stroke the ball with a forehand groundstroke before it hits the ground. In the act of serving, if you allow the ball to touch the ground before making contact, a fault would be called.

Fig. 23.2 Beginner's underhand service. Only use an underhand motion if you are unable to execute the normal overhead service with accuracy.

23.2B   Service follow-through.

23.2A   Ready to start beginner's underhand service.

DRILLS FOR INTERMEDIATES

With the basic forehand, backhand, and service firmly grooved, you are now ready to travel the exciting road to mastery of the game. You will enjoy learning new strokes that will make you a more complete player.

Drill

LEARNING THE SLICE

WHAT IS A SLICE?

A slice is a stroke that produces underspin and sidespin on the ball. The forward swing of the slice is usually in a high-to-low direction, and at contact, the lower edge of the racket face is leading the top edge. Groundstrokes are often sliced, while volleys should always be hit with slice action.

WIPE THE BALL

To understand the slice action, grasp a ball in your left hand, while holding your racket with the forehand grip a foot to the right with the racket face slightly above the ball. Contact the ball in a wiping action with your racket strings, and firmly hold the ball without releasing it (Fig. 24.1). Do fifteen slice wipes on the forehand, and then fifteen on the backhand.

Fig. 24.1   Wipe the ball with the racket strings to learn slice. Wiping the ball with the backhand slice on the left, and wiping with forehand slice on the right.

BUMPING BALL IN AIR
WITH SLICE ACTION

An effective technique to learn to slice the ball is to bump a ball in the air by undercutting the ball with the racket. Make the ball spin rapidly by using a considerable amount of hand-wrist movement. In a stationary position, first practice your forehand, and then your backhand (Fig. 25.1). Be able to bump-slice five consecutive balls off both sides before proceeding to the next exercise.

Fig. 25.1 Bumping up balls with slice action. Bumping the ball with forehand slice on the left, and bumping the ball with backhand slice on the right.

Drill **26**

GROUNDSTROKE SLICE FROM A SELF-DROPPED BALL

Slices are easily controlled, especially on the backhand, and add variety to a player's repertoire. Slices can be effective as a method of advancing to the net (approach shots). Practice dropping a ball to the ground, and slicing it to a fence with the forehand (Figs. 26.1A–C) and then the backhand (Figs. 26.2A–C) from a distance of twenty-five feet. When you can hit the fence ten consecutive times off both sides, begin the next exercise.

Fig. 26.1   Slicing a forehand from a self-dropped ball.

26.1B Contacting the ball with forehand slice. Racket swing is from high to low with lower edge of racket head leading the stroke.

26.1A   Ready to slice. Racket head is high.

26.1C   Holding follow-through.

Fig. 26.2 Slicing a backhand from a self-dropped ball.

26.2A Ready to slice. Weight is now on back foot, and racket head is high.

26.2C Holding follow-through. Weight is now on forward foot.

26.2B Contacting ball with backhand slice.

Drill 27

GROUNDSTROKE SLICE FROM A TOSSED BALL

With your racket fully back on the forehand side, a partner tosses you a ball underhand from twenty feet away. After one bounce, slowly slice the ball back to your partner and hold the follow-through for a couple of seconds (Fig. 27.1). Do not move your feet; just transfer your weight from back to front foot. A *very* slow and accurate toss is essential. Next, start slicing with the backhand from a stationary position (Fig. 27.2). After developing accuracy in slicing while standing still, have your partner slowly toss balls a few feet away so that you will slice on the move.

Fig. 27.1 Hitting a forehand slice from a tossed ball. Tossed ball should bounce halfway between tosser and hitter.

Fig. 27.2 Ready to hit a backhand slice from a tossed ball.

Drill 28

GROUNDSTROKE SLICE RALLYING ON BACKBOARD

Stand eight feet from the wall, and start a rally using backhand and forehand slices. As you become proficient, move to a distance of twenty feet from the backboard (Fig. 28). Take balls on the first bounce, vary your pace, and count consecutive hits in the target area.

Fig. 28 Groundstroke slice rallying on backboard.

Drill

SHORT RALLYING GAME USING ENTIRE FORECOURT

FORECOURT RALLYING

Standing behind the service line, start a rally with your partner by bouncing and stroking the ball anyplace in his forecourt (service boxes) (Fig. 29.1). Use slices and drives with forehands and backhands and move your partner as much as possible. Control is stressed by using a slow and short swing.

Fig. 29.1 Rallying and playing points in forecourt area.

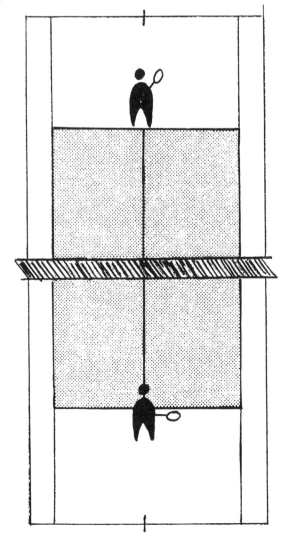

PLAYING FORECOURT GAME

After rallying in the forecourt, you may start playing games. Standing behind the service line, bounce and stroke the ball anyplace within your partner's forecourt. Whoever wishes may put the ball in play for the first and succeeding points. Take all balls after the first bounce using forehands and backhands. The game ends and a new one begins when a player has ten points (Fig. 29.2).

Fig. 29.2 Playing forecourt game.

Drill **30**

VOLLEY READINESS DRILL

To prepare for the volley, toss a ball back and forth to a partner, using an underhand motion (Figs. 30A and B). The catch will take place as far out in front of the body as possible. Step forward with the left foot on the forehand volley just as you catch the ball with the right hand. Partners stand twenty feet from each other. The toss should be slow and deliberate and should not begin until the target (partner's racket hand) is up and ready for the catch. Toss and catch twenty balls before continuing to the next exercise where the racket is introduced.

Fig. 30 Tossing and catching a ball to prepare for forehand volley.

30A Tossing to racket hand used as forehand volley target.

30B Catching ball to simulate forehand volley. Left foot hits ground at same time right hand catches ball.

Drill **31**

FOREHAND VOLLEY DRILL

The one-grip method (Continental or Australian) is the most desirable grip for volleying since you do not have to make a change. However, there are fine volleyers who do change grips.

HIGH FOREHAND VOLLEY

With your racket extended for a high forehand volley, your partner slowly tosses a ball from twenty feet away. Volley the ball to your partner using an undercut or slice racket action, and he will catch the ball on the fly. Before the ball is tossed, the hitter should be in the ready position with the racket (target) up so the stroke will not be rushed (Figs. 31.1 A and B). On all forehand volleys, lay the wrist back toward the forearm, as far as possible, to enable you to meet the ball well in front of the body. The volley should be slowly sliced toward the chest of your partner. Do this exercise against the fence since it prevents a backswing. Practice the drill until you have gained accuracy.

Fig. 31.1   High forehand volley drill.

31.1A   Ready to toss with racket in front of body as target.

31.1B   Slice high forehand volley. A very short racket backswing and follow-through are used on volleys.

LOW FOREHAND VOLLEY

The instructions for the low forehand volley are basically the same as those for the high forehand, except the volleyer places the head of his racket at knee height (Figs. 31.2A and B). The racket head is higher than the hand since this position offers a solid hand–wrist foundation to execute a firm volley.

Fig. 31.2   Low forehand volley drill. Volleyer's knees are bent.

31.2A   Ready to toss to low forehand volley target. Racket head should be higher than hand unless ball is *very* low.

31.2B   Slice low forehand volley. Grip can be Eastern forehand or, preferably, Continental. Make sure the racket contacts ball at same time left foot touches the ground.

Drill 32

BACKHAND VOLLEY DRILL

HIGH BACKHAND VOLLEY

Follow the same instructions as the high forehand volley in Drill 31, substituting backhand for forehand (Figs. 32.1A and B). The Continental or Australian grip should be used on the backhand volley.

Fig. 32.1 High backhand volley drill.

32.1A   Ready to toss with racket in front of body as target.

32.1B   Slice high backhand volley. Weight is transferred to forward foot on all volleys.

LOW BACKHAND VOLLEY

Follow the same instructions as the low forehand volley in Drill 31, substituting the backhand for forehand (Figs. 32.2A and B).

Fig. 32.2   Low backhand volley drill.

32.2A   Ready to toss to low backhand volley target.

32.2B   Slice low backhand volley.

BACKHAND VOLLEY FOR BALL HIT STRAIGHT AT
YOU

When a ball is coming directly at you, take it with the
backhand volley, and place your body weight toward
the direction you are hitting (Figs. 32.3A and B). The
inside of your right shoulder is the dividing line between
balls taken as backhand volleys and those volleyed as
forehands (Fig. 32.4).

In the rare instance when there is a considerable
amount of time to volley a ball, it is wise to take it with
the strongest stroke. Like running around a backhand
groundstroke and taking it with the forehand, running
around a backhand or forehand volley can also be
effective.

**Fig. 32.3 Use the backhand volley for a ball
coming straight at you.**

32.3A Ready to toss the ball slowly and directly
toward volleyer's chest.

32.3B Slicing ball coming toward chest with
backhand volley.

Fig. 32.4   Determining when to use the forehand or backhand volley.

Forehand Volley Territory   Backhand Volley Territory

Drill 33

VOLLEY AND RECOVERY PRACTICE WITHOUT A BALL

Footwork for the volley can be developed without using a ball by repeatedly practicing the aforementioned volley motions. You can do this by yourself, or an instructor or partner can call out one of five volley actions to you. These are high or low forehand volley, high or low backhand volley, or ball hit at you.

The player starts in the ready position with the racket head held high (Fig. 33A). He then quickly volleys (Fig. 33B), and recovers to his original ready position (Fig. 33C). Fifteen consecutive volley and recovery acts, without the ball, should be performed. This drill, like certain other drills in this book, should be practiced often until it becomes automatic.

Fig. 33   Volley and recovery drill.

33B   ''Hit a high backhand volley.'' Player simulates high backhand volley motion, without ball.

33C   ''Recover.'' Volleyer quickly recovers to original, or ready position, and awaits the next command.

33A   Player in ready position for volley and awaiting command. The racket head should be held high when in the ready position for the volley. The coach says: ''Ready.''

Drill 34

ALTERNATE FOREHAND AND BACKHAND VOLLEYS

Standing with your back to the fence, and the tosser twenty feet away, you are given alternate volleys: first you hit the forehand high volley, then backhand, then forehand, etc. Your partner should not rush you; he tosses the ball only when he sees your racket (target) up in the ball contact position. The drill should proceed slowly and deliberately.

Drill **35**

VOLLEYING WHEN TOSSED-BALL DIRECTION IS UNKNOWN

Standing on opposite sides of the net and twenty-five feet from you, a partner slowly tosses you balls in various directions. He gives low and high forehands and backhands, as well as balls aimed directly at you. Volley the ball to your partner who catches it on the fly. Wait in the ready position to see the direction of the tossed ball, since it comes unannounced. When you gain mastery over balls tossed close to you, your partner can direct balls four or five feet away.

Drill 36

DEEP VOLLEYING

With your partner standing a yard behind his baseline, and you standing between your service line and the net, rally the ball back and forth. Your partner takes your volley after the first bounce and strokes it back to you. Partners should aim the balls toward each other. Attempt to volley all balls between the service and baselines (Fig. 36.1). The groundstroker will return the balls as low over the net as possible to strengthen his defense against a net rusher (Fig. 36.2). Exchange places with your partner periodically.

Fig. 36.1 Diagram showing backcourt area where all volleys should land.

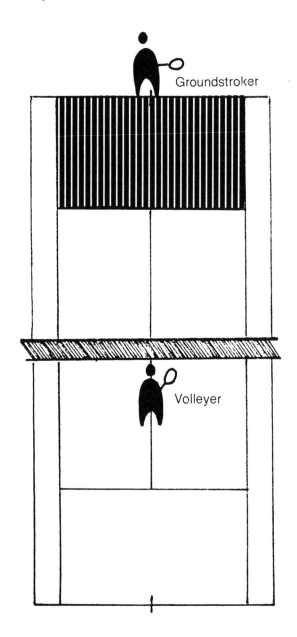

Groundstroker

Volleyer

Fig. 36.2   Low net clearance is used by baseliner in deep volleying drill.

Drill **37**

LEARNING TO SPLIT STOP

When the advance is made from backcourt to the net (volleying) position, it is recommended that a split stop be used to slow down and gain balance. A split stop is simply coming down on both feet at the same time after a run.

From a split stop you can take one, two, or three steps and volley a ball, or hit an overhead. The only time a split stop is not used is when an opponent hits a very slow, high ball that you can volley without breaking stride. Do a split stop in hopscotch manner (Fig. 37.1). Try not to hop too high off the ground. Next, run from the baseline to the service box, split stop, and pretend you are hitting a forehand volley (Fig. 37.2).

Fig. 37.1 Practice the hopscotch split stop.

Spilt stop in which both feet land at same time.

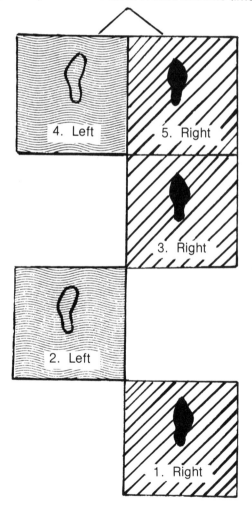

Fig. 37.2 Combining the run, split stop, and volley (without ball).

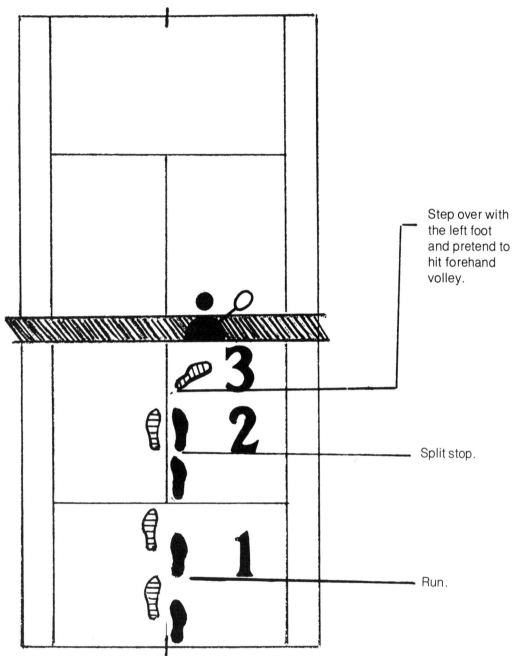

Step over with
the left foot
and pretend to
hit forehand
volley.

Split stop.

Run.

Drill 38

SPLIT STOP AND VOLLEY THE BALL

Do the same run and split stop that you just performed on the court, and a ball will be tossed to your forehand side which you will volley right after you split stop. Make sure your body is well balanced as you volley the ball.

The tosser will stand in the opposite service court, about twenty-five feet away from where the volleyer will contact the ball. The toss will be slow and careful. After doing the run, split stop, and forehand volley a number of times, then switch to the backhand (Fig. 38).

Fig. 38   Split stop before volleying a tossed ball. Volleyer will turn and step out with right foot as ball is contacted on backhand side. In a game situation, split stop just as your opponent is about to hit the ball.

Drill **39**

OVERHEAD SMASH FROM A SELF-TOSSED BALL

The proper smash action contains two key elements: a good racket drop, and a short backswing. The overhead smash is exactly like the simple service (Figs. 21.3A–E). As the lob comes down, the smasher waits with racket pointing straight up in the air. The racket head is then dropped behind the back and the swing is made.

Fig. 39.1 Half-court target for intermediate overhead smash.

FOREHAND SMASH

Standing just inside the service line, you will toss a ball fifteen feet above you and slightly behind you, and smash it toward either the left or right side of the opposite court (Figs. 39.1 and 39.2). Smash thirty or forty times, or until you can master the stroke easily.

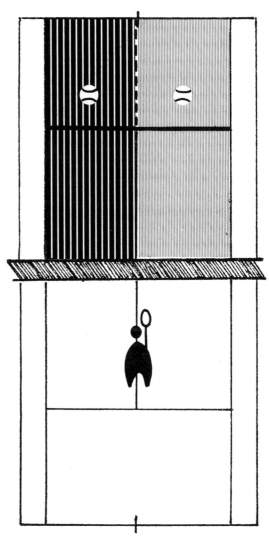

Always aim toward target area (⊖), not down the middle of court.

Fig. 39.2 Ready to hit a forehand smash from a self-tossed ball. Do not allow tossed ball to bounce before hitting it.

FOREHAND SMASH FROM A BOUNCING BALL

Next, standing on the service line, toss the ball twenty-five feet in the air directly above. Let the ball bounce, and smash it to the left or right side of the opposite court (Fig. 39.3). Do this bouncing overhead drill twenty times.

Fig. 39.3 Hitting forehand smash from bouncing ball. Toss ball very high and allow it to bounce once before smashing.

BACKHAND SMASH

Hit ten or fifteen backhand overheads in the same manner as the forehand smash which was hit before the ball bounced (Fig. 39.4). Avoid the backhand overhead as much as possible by running quickly to your left and using the forehand. However this can be extremely difficult when dealing with quick, low lobs aimed at the backhand side.

FURTHER OVERHEAD DEVELOPMENT

As you become more proficient in smashing, toss the ball higher and further behind, in order to challenge yourself more. Force yourself to move back faster. Practicing serves is an indirect but worthwhile method of strengthening the overhead.

Fig. 39.4   Hitting a backhand smash from a self-tossed ball. Do not allow tossed ball to bounce before hitting it.

Drill **40**

OVERHEAD PRACTICE ON BACKBOARD

FOREHAND SMASH

The overhead smash can be developed on a backboard as well as a tennis court. Standing ten to twelve feet from a backboard, hit the ball to the ground causing it to bounce between you and the barrier. The ball then rebounds against the backboard and goes high above your head, where you smash it toward the target on the wall (Figs. 40.1A–C). Practice this drill until you are accurate.

Fig. 40.1   Developing the smash on a backboard.

40.1B   Setup shot is hit firmly to ground so it will rebound high off wall forcing player to stretch.

40.1A   About to hit ball to ground to set up the smash.

40.1C   Player smashes rebounding ball to target area.

BACKHAND SMASH

The setup for the backhand overhead is made the same way as the forehand. This smash is also directed toward the wall target.

FOREHAND SMASH FROM A BOUNCING BALL

A high backboard is necessary to develop the bouncing forehand smash. Lob by slowly stroking or tossing a ball high (twelve or thirteen feet) against a wall, allow it to bounce, then smash the ball toward a target (Figs. 40.2A–D).

Fig. 40.2 Smashing bouncing lob to backboard.

40.2A Drill begins with high lob toward backboard. The upper target is the lob target, and the lower target is for smashing.

40.2B Lob rebounds off backboard to ground as player starts turning sideways to get into position for smashing.

40.2C Ball rebounds high off ground and is about to be smashed.

40.2D Overhead smash is aimed directly at lower target.

Drill **41**

LEARNING THE OFFENSIVE LOB

A good offensive lob is a slowly stroked ball aimed slightly above and beyond the reach of a player. This lob denies the opponent sufficient time to run back and retrieve the ball once it is over his head. The offensive lob must be disguised, and up to the split second before the hit (or lift) the backswing should appear as a groundstroke.

LOBBING OFFENSIVELY FROM A SELF-DROPPED BALL

Standing at your service line with your partner in the opposite court six feet from the net, drop a ball to the ground, and lob it a yard or two above his outstretched racket (Fig. 41.1). This exercise may also be done on a backboard with a partner standing against the wall.

Fig. 41.1   Stroking a forehand offensive lob from a self-dropped ball. Lobber's weight has been transferred from back to front foot. Aim offensive lobs over net person's backhand side.

LOBBING OFFENSIVELY FROM A TOSSED BALL

Standing inside your service line, with a partner on the opposite side of the net standing inside his service line, you will execute an offensive lob from a tossed ball with the forehand and then the backhand (Fig. 41.2). After the partner tosses you a ball, he can extend his racket overhead enabling you to see how high to lob. This, too, may be done on a backboard with a partner standing against the wall.

Fig. 41.2 Stroking a backhand offensive lob from a tossed ball. Backhand lob is usually hit with slice (backspin) action.

OFFENSIVE LOB RALLYING ON A COURT

An effective way to learn the offensive lob is to initiate a lob rally with your partner from baseline to baseline (Fig. 41.3). You may lob down the line, crosscourt, or down the middle of the court. On clay courts many good players will lob offensively toward their opponent's backhand when he is in the backcourt. A high ball to the backhand is difficult to hit.

Fig. 41.3   Offensive lob rallying on a court.

OFFENSIVE LOB RALLYING ON BACKBOARD

If you have a high backboard or wall, start an offensive lob rally, using both the forehand and backhand. If you aim toward a target, or some kind of mark, your practice will be especially beneficial (Fig. 41.4).

Fig. 41.4 Offensive lob rallying on a backboard. Aim lob to high target.

Drill  42

LEARNING THE DEFENSIVE LOB

The defensive lob is used when you are caught deep behind the baseline and have little chance of passing the netman with a groundstroke. This lob is aimed high, deep, and down the middle of the opponent's court.

LOBBING DEFENSIVELY FROM A SELF-DROPPED BALL

Standing slightly behind the baseline, bounce the ball and lob it as high as you can to the opposite court (Fig. 42.1). Lob about ten forehands and ten backhands or as many as it takes to gain accuracy.

Fig. 42.1 Lobbing defensively from a self-dropped ball. Bend low and lob high to allow ample time to recover to a better court position.

LOBBING DEFENSIVELY FROM A TOSSED BALL

Standing behind the baseline, lob a tossed ball as high as possible toward the opposite court. Your partner, standing on the same side of the court as you but near the service line, slowly tosses you a ball underhand (Fig. 42.2). Lob fifteen forehands and fifteen backhands or as many as necessary to master the stroke.

Fig. 42.2 Lobbing defensively from a tossed ball. The higher the lob goes, the faster it comes down, making a high lob difficult to smash.

Drill **43**

LOB AND OVERHEAD
DRILL

Stand near the service line of your court while your partner, standing near one singles sideline of the court or the other, sends up lobs from his baseline. He hits either offensive or defensive lobs to anyplace in your court. Smash the lobs directly at your partner so that a rally can be established using lobs and overheads. After doing the drill for ten or fifteen minutes, switch roles.

Drill **44**

LEARNING THE HALF VOLLEY

A *half volley* is a misnomer. It is not a volley, but a groundstroke in which the racket contacts the ball immediately after it hits the ground. It could be termed a "quick pickup" since the ball is taken on the rise. A half volley can be distinguished from other groundstrokes because the sound of the racket striking the ball occurs immediately after the sound of the ball hitting the ground. Listen for this double sound. A correct half volley is executed with the top of the racket no higher than two feet from the ground.

HALF-VOLLEYING FROM A SELF-DROPPED BALL

Standing eight feet from the wall, drop a ball, and with a very short backswing hit the ball immediately after it strikes the ground (Figs. 44.1A and B). Stroke twenty balls with the forehand and the same number with the backhand. If you prefer, you may direct the half volley to a partner, rather than the backboard.

Fig. 44.1   Half-volleying from a self-dropped ball.

44.1A   Ready to hit half volley.

44.1B   Stroke ball to target using short forward swing and no backswing. Hit once, then catch and redrop the ball for a second hit.

HALF-VOLLEYING FROM A TOSSED BALL

Standing eight feet from your partner who will toss the ball, hold your racket ready a foot behind the spot where the tossed ball will hit the ground. Half-volley the ball back to your partner (Figs. 44.2A and B). A very slow and accurate toss is essential. Fifty forehand and fifty backhand half volleys should be practiced.

HALF-VOLLEY RALLY ON WALL

Standing six feet from a backboard, softly hit half volleys off the forehand and backhand. Keep a rally going as long as possible.

Fig. 44.2   Half-volleying from a tossed ball.

44.2A   Ready for the toss. A slow toss is made so that ball will bounce near point X.

44.2B   End of half-volley stroke with tosser catching ball. Keep knees bent throughout stroke.

Drill **45**

INTERMEDIATE VOLLEYING DRILLS ON BACKBOARD

Volley practice on a backboard is very valuable since great numbers of balls are stroked in a short period of time. Specific weaknesses can be corrected. Since securing a practice court is sometimes difficult (and costly) and arranging tennis dates can be time consuming, this can be an efficient method of improving your game.

VOLLEY RALLYING ON BACKBOARD

Standing three or four yards from the wall, start a rally by volleying as many consecutive balls as possible. Maintain control by not overhitting, and, of course, do not allow balls to hit the ground. This is excellent practice to learn a fast grip change for those players who have elected the two-grip method.

VOLLEY RALLYING INTO BACKBOARD TARGET

Standing fifteen feet from the wall, and aiming at a target four feet high, try to sustain a volley rally (Fig. 45.1). This drill is designed to improve the low volley, and it forces you to increase pace. Use minimal foot movement in this drill.

Fig. 45.1 Volleying into a backboard target from fifteen feet. Try to sustain a rally in this challenging low-volley drill.

VOLLEYING CLOSE TO BACKBOARD

This is a drill to sharpen the reflexes necessary for a quick volley. Standing six feet from the wall, volley the ball and attempt to maintain a rally (Fig. 45.2).

Fig. 45.2   Close-volleying at backboard. Use one grip, if possible.

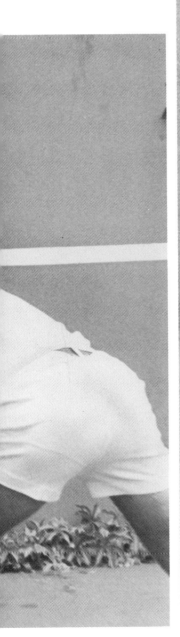

Drill **46**

COMBINED DRIVE AND SLICE PRACTICE ON BACKBOARD

STROKING DRIVES AND SLICES TOWARD A TARGET

In this drill, stand twenty-five feet from the backboard, and integrate drives and slices, using forehands and backhands (Fig. 46.1). Hit most balls when they are at their peak after bouncing or at waist level. Occasionally take the ball on the rise and drive it hard, as a tournament player would on a passing shot.

Aim the balls into the target and direct the passing shots low, a foot above the net line. Sometimes, slice the backhand very low and slow, using it like a dink shot as you would when an opponent comes to the net.

Fig. 46.1 Stroking drives and slices toward a backboard target. The lower half of the target is for passing shots.

STROKING ON THE MOVE, USING A PAIR
OF BACKBOARD TARGETS

When you are confident of your ability to handle
stationary drives and slices, try stroking on the move.
Tape two, one-foot-square pieces of paper four feet
apart on the wall, and four feet from the ground.
Alternate stroking the ball to one target and then to the
other. In those instances when you are drawn extremely wide to one side or the other, aim for the target
nearest you since hitting the distant target would end
the rally (Fig. 46.2).

Fig. 46.2   Getting movement on drives and slices by stroking to a pair of backboard targets.

LOB-OVERHEAD DRILL ON HIGH WALL

This is a valuable drill, but requires a high (fourteen foot) backboard. Start by bouncing and lobbing a ball toward a lob target, or high mark on a wall (Fig. 47.1A). Let it bounce after coming off the wall, and then smash the ball toward the lower target (Fig. 47.1B). After the ball rebounds from the lower target, let it bounce once, and lob it again toward the upper target. Continue this cycle using both forehand and backhand lobs.

Fig. 47.1 Lob-overhead drill on high wall.

47.1A   Aiming toward the lob target. Body weight has been transferred from back to front foot. The upper target is for lobs, and the lower target is for smashes.

GROUNDSTROKING LOBS

Once in a while groundstroke the lobbed ball to the lower target with the forehand or backhand (Fig. 47.2).

Fig. 47.2   Hitting a high groundstroke off the lob.

47.1B Smashing toward the low target. Assume position sideways to target when getting ready to hit an overhead smash.

PRACTICING INTERMEDIATE SERVICE ON BACKBOARD

Standing forty feet from the wall, serve fifty balls toward a one-square-yard target (Fig. 48). The following is a list of checkpoint questions that should be answered in the affirmative:

1. Is the racket being dropped as far down the back as possible? (See Fig. 21.1.)
2. Is the front foot remaining still during the serve?
3. Are you reaching as high as you can?
4. Are you watching the ball as you hit it?
5. Does your weight continue forward in the direction of the shot after contacting the ball?

Fig. 48 Practicing the intermediate service on a backboard. Check yourself for the following: (1) front foot stationary, (2) reaching high, (3) watching ball, and (4) body weight moving in direction of service.

Drill **49**

PRACTICING INTERMEDIATE SERVICE ON COURT

Practice serving by yourself, or have a friend return your serves. Accumulate fifty to one hundred balls and use an apron or a stand so that you will not spend time or energy in bending over to pick up a small number of balls. Do not serve more than 300 balls at one session, and allow three or four hours of arm rest if you practice more than once a day. Do not serve more than 600 balls in a day. Mentally divide each service court into two halves and aim for one of them (Fig. 49.1).

Fig. 49.1 Intermediate serving targets and serving positions.

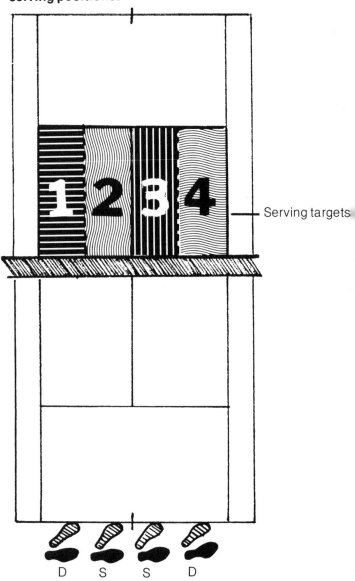

Serving targets

Serving positions for singles (S) and doubles (D). When serving from the singles and doubles positions on the left side of the center mark, aim for boxes 3 and 4. When serving from the right side of the center mark, aim for boxes 1 and 2.

Put variety into your serving sessions. Practice serving from the singles and doubles positions (Fig. 49.2) into the right and left service courts, into the wind and with the wind, and looking into the sun and having the sun at your back. Occasionally, practice running to the service line after you serve and do a split stop. If you are unsure of the split stop, refer to Drill 37.

Fig. 49.2   Position for serving into the ad (left) court in singles. Converted kitchen apron holds 20 balls.

LEARNING THE CONTINENTAL SERVICE GRIP

Fig. 50.1 Tapping gently on fence with Continental grip. Notice the wrist angle used when hitting a flat service with a Continental grip. In this drill, use only a one foot backswing as indicated on photo by arrows.

You should become familiar with the Continental or advanced serving grip as this grip is the most conducive to placing spin on service. This grip is illustrated in "Drills for Beginners" (Figs. 2.2A and B). The Continental grip is used by advanced players because it can produce a wide variety of serves and offers safety potential through overspin and slice.

In this drill you will develop feel for the Continental grip on the flat and slice service actions. Using the Continental grip, lightly tap the head of the racket against a fence in order to feel the wrist angle for the Continental flat serve (Fig. 50.1). Secondly, bounce the ball to the ground 100 times to become more accustomed to the Continental grip (Fig. 50.2).

If you lack serving power do not spend time making the transition to this grip since you will not need spin to control your serve—gravity will pull the ball down into the court. If you have an abundant supply of power, but lack control, this service grip is ideal.

Fig. 50.2 Becoming familiar with the spin serve by bouncing a ball to the ground with slice action, using the Continental grip. Right edge of racket head is nearest ground.

LEARNING THE SLICE AND OVERSPIN SERVES

Serves hit with spin have greater control since the racket strings ''grab'' the ball. Slice serves can move an opponent out of court, leaving an opening for your next shot (Fig. 51.1). Overspin serves have a safety margin since the forward spinning ball drops faster than other serves after passing over the net (Fig. 51.2). Spin serves also produce changes of pace, lessening the possibility of a player achieving adequate timing to make a good return of service.

Fig. 51.1   Effect of slice service on a court.

Path of flat service showing the widest it can draw the opponent off court.

Path of slice service which will draw the receiver out of position. —

Slice service creates opening here for the server's first groundstroke.

Sidespin direction of slice service.

Fig. 51.2   Effect of overspin service on a court. The overspin service has a greater safety margin over the net than the flat service.

Overspin Service

Flat Service

LEARNING THE SLICE SERVICE
BY CHOKING UP ON GRIP

Stand sideways, five feet from a fence or wall, and choke up on the racket (holding it above the leather) with the Continental grip. Using little backswing, give the ball a glancing hit on its upper right front—at two o'clock if you picture the face of a clock on the ball. This action produces sidespin or slice. If done correctly, the ball will bounce slightly to the player's right after hitting the fence (Figs. 51.3A–C). Slice twenty serves to the fence.

Fig. 51.3   Learning the slice service by choking up on the racket with Continental grip.

51.3A   Ready to toss.

51.3B   Slicing ball. (Picture the ball as a clock and stroke the ball with slice at two o'clock.)

51.3C Finish. Ball should rebound slightly to right after hitting fence.

SLICE SERVING TO FENCE AND ON COURT

After successfully slicing with the choked-up grip, hit twenty serves to the fence by correctly holding the racket on the leather using the Continental grip. Finally, practice serving on a court, and attempt to get the ball to break slightly to your left, as a slice should. (A slice rebounds in a different direction on a court than against a fence.) Toss the ball slightly to your right in order to slice with authority.

LEARNING THE OVERSPIN SERVICE BY CHOKING UP ON GRIP

The overspin serve is more difficult to learn than the slice. Stand sideways, five feet from a fence or wall, and choke up on the racket using the Continental grip. Toss the ball above and in front of you, and brush or wipe the back of the ball with the racket strings in an upward motion (Figs. 51.4A–D). If you make contact correctly, the ball will jump up slightly after hitting the fence. You can recognize the correct movement by taking your racket hand and brushing the back of your head with an upward stroke.

OVERSPIN SERVING TO FENCE AND ON COURT

After successfully learning overspin by choking up on the racket, serve twenty balls to the fence by correctly holding the racket on the leather, still using the Continental grip. Lastly, practice serving on a court with overspin, tossing the ball slightly to your left.

Fig. 51.4 Learning the overspin service by choking up on the racket with Continental grip.

51.4A   Ready to toss.

51.4B   Tossing ball with slight racket drop behind head.

51.4C   Make contact by brushing back of ball upward.

51.4D   Finish. Ball should rebound slightly upward
after hitting fence.

Drill 52

HAND, WRIST, AND FOREARM STRENGTHENING EXERCISE

An effective method of strengthening hand, wrist, and forearm muscles is to practice with the cover on your racket for three or four minutes after your regular workout. You can do this on a court or backboard (Fig. 52).

Fig. 52   Stroking with cover on racket to strengthen muscles. Strength promotes power and control.

Drill 53

PICTURING STROKES MENTALLY

Physical educators have proved that forming a mental image of a stroke can be a valuable learning exercise. It is a method of overlearning and grooving a skill. Although this technique does not have the excitement of an actual playing situation, it can be challenging.

In a quiet atmosphere, while sitting or lying down, form a mental picture of each of your strokes from the backswing to completion (Fig. 53). Visualize each stroke ten times. Discover which strokes you can picture with clarity, and which are difficult to imagine. Attempt to strengthen the mental picture of all of your strokes.

Fig. 53 Forming a mental picture of a tennis stroke.

ADVANCED AND TOURNAMENT-LEVEL DRILLS

Now that you have learned the rudiments of most of the tennis strokes, you will have the opportunity to practice them until you gain shot mastery. See if you can meet the challenges offered by these drills.

Drill  **54**

MUSCLE-STRENGTHENING EXERCISES

When muscles are strong, quickness of body movement can be achieved. Powerful wrist and forearm muscles add firmness to stroke production. Here are some muscle strengthening exercises that many champions use:

GRIP-STRENGTHENING EXERCISES

Squeezing a squash ball or handball often is a good hand and wrist strength developer. Using a V-shaped or rectangular spring-operated strengthening device is helpful (Fig. 54.1), as is squeezing a tennis ball for a few minutes. These grip-strengthening exercises are more fun if done with the pronounced beat of lively music.

Fig. 54.1 Squeeze device to strengthen hand, wrist, and forearm. Squeeze 15 times, then hold closed for 15 seconds, and repeat this sequence.

133

STOMACH-STRENGTHENING EXERCISE

Performing sit-ups on a daily or triweekly basis is good for your stomach and lower back (Figs. 54. 2A-1 and 2). If you have had lower back difficulty, it is advisable that you do sit-ups with bent knees (Figs. 54.2B-1 and 2).

Fig. 54.2 Sit-up exercises to strengthen stomach muscles. Do 20 rapid sit-ups daily.

54.2A-1   Straight-knee sit-up exercise. Ready to begin.

54.2B-1   Bent-knee sit-up exercise. Ready to begin.

54.2A-2   Touch right knee with left elbow. Return to prone position, then touch left knee with right elbow.

54.2B-2   Touch right knee with left elbow. Return to ready position, then touch left knee with right elbow.

HAND-ARM-SHOULDER EXERCISE

Regular push-ups, or push-ups from the finger tips, will strengthen the hands, arms, and shoulders (Fig. 54.3).

Fig. 54.3 Doing push-ups to strengthen hands, arms, and shoulders. One push-up consists of touching the floor with your chest, and then straightening the arms, keeping the back straight. Try to do 15 push-ups daily, or every other day. Push-ups can be done on finger tips, as below, or on palm of hand.

LEG-STRENGTHENING EXERCISE

Knees-to-chest (kangaroo) jumps strengthen leg muscles and give a player greater spring. This is also a great conditioning exercise (Fig. 54.4).

Fig. 54.4 Doing knees-to-chest ("kangaroo") jumps to strengthen legs. Jump up in the air and touch your knees to your chest. Do 10 knee-to-chest jumps daily. (If you can do 30 in a row you are in superb condition.)

Drill **55**

EXERCISES FOR SPEED, ENDURANCE, AND MOBILITY

For the serious-minded player, running exercises are invaluable. The higher the level of play, the faster are its players. Running is a quick conditioner; you can get into shape more rapidly by running than by playing tennis (Fig. 55.1).

Fig. 55.1 Running to improve speed and stamina.

The following are good leg exercises:

RUNNING IN PLACE

If you do not have a track or field nearby, running in place can be an adequate substitute (Fig. 55.2).

BICYCLING ON BACK

If you have little available time or live in a confining city apartment house, you can exercise by lying on your back and practice bicycling (Fig. 55.3). A player with a foot injury can stay in condition this way. A few minutes of this exercise is helpful.

Fig. 55.2 Running in place and bringing knees up to touch hands.

Fig. 55.3 Bicycle exercise. Move your legs up and down in a circle as you would on a bicycle.

RUNNING UP STAIRS

This is a great conditioner. Running up a flight of stairs and walking back down several times in succession will improve fitness (Fig. 55.4).

SPRINTING

Doing a dozen 100-yard dashes after you have played three sets of tennis takes willpower, but they will improve speed and conditioning. Periodic jogging from two to five miles is good for the legs and the cardiovascular system; it can also be relaxing. Sprinting, however, is more valuable for competitive tennis.

Fig. 55.4 Running up flights of stairs. Do not attempt to run *down* stairs—it is dangerous.

RUNNING BACKWARDS

Try a half-dozen thirty-yard bursts, running backwards. This exercise promotes tennis court mobility.

SHUFFLING SIDEWAYS

The shuffle step (see Drills for Beginners, Figs. 14.1 and 14.2), frequently employed on the tennis court, should be practiced quickly. Do this exercise for a minute or two during each training session.

TENNIS COURT MOVEMENT EXERCISE

This diagrammed movement drill combines forward sprinting, backward running, and sideway shuffle stepping. Four to six round trips are recommended (Fig. 55.5).

Fig. 55.5   Tennis court movement exercise.

Key

|| Running forward to net.

.... Skipping sideways facing net.

||| Running backward from net.

Starting and ending point for one round trip.

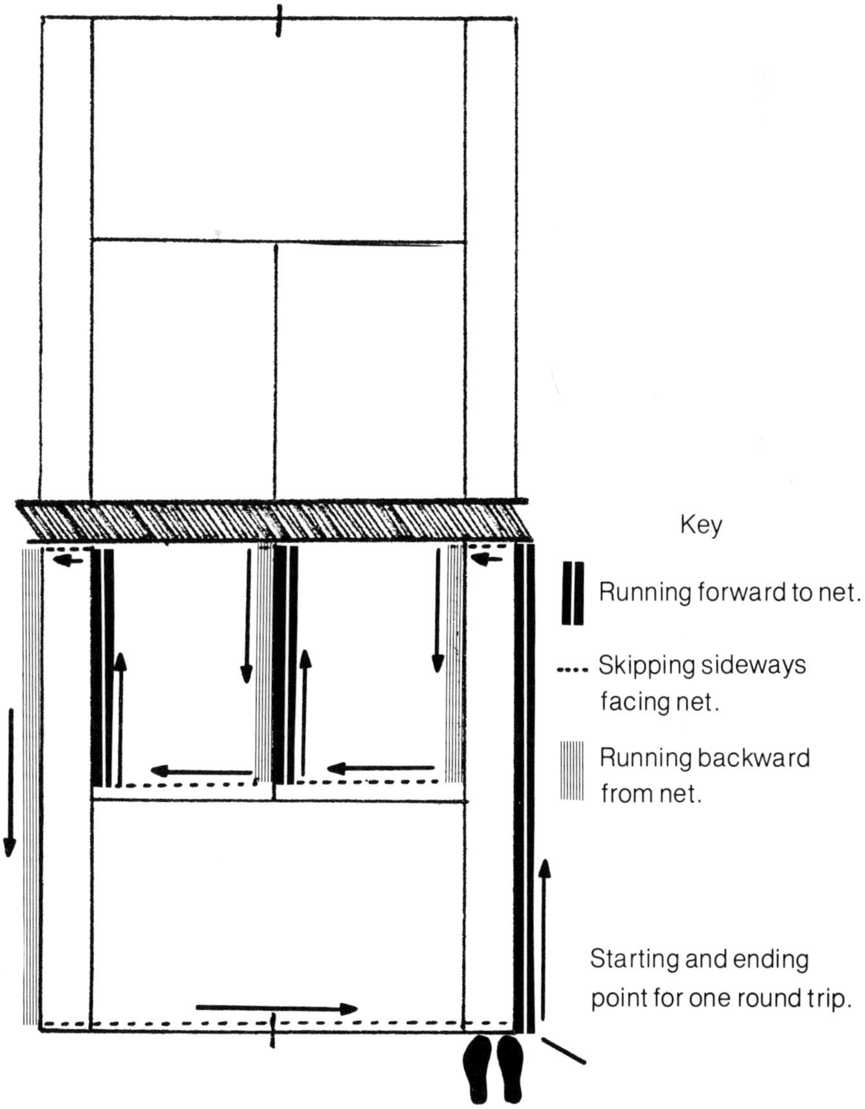

Drill **56**

SOLO AND SHADOW TENNIS: CONDITIONING EXERCISES

SOLO TENNIS

If you would like to have a strenuous workout, try solo tennis, practicing footwork and stroke action as in a match but without a ball. For example, serve, then volley, then smash, run back to the baseline, hit a drive from your forehand corner, then backhand corner, and run for a dropshot near the net on your forehand side.

SHADOW TENNIS

In this exercise there is a leader, and a follower who is the shadow. Both are on the same side of the net and are facing the net. The follower runs in the same direction as the leader and executes the same stroke. The shadow stays five yards behind the leader at all times (Fig. 56).

Fig. 56 Shadow tennis. Follower copies the leader and stays five yards behind to avoid a collision.

Drill 57

OVERHEAD–TOUCH NET DRILL

This drill develops a player's ability to go back quickly and smash lobs. It is also a conditioner. A partner, feeding you lobs, stands in the center of the court behind the opposite baseline. You smash his lobs from the forecourt area (Fig. 57.A), rush up and touch

Fig. 57 Overhead–touch net drill.

57A   Overhead is aimed to baseliner.

the net with your racket (Fig. 57.B), go quickly back and spring up to make the next smash, then touch the net and repeat the whole sequence.

Aim all overheads directly toward the lobber so a rally can be established. Repeat this exercise until you are tired. You should have at least ten or fifteen balls available so little time will be spent picking them up.

57B   Smasher runs up and touches net as baseliner lobs next ball to smasher.

Drill **58**
SMASH BOUNCING LOB DRILL

SMASH BOUNCING LOBS INTO DOUBLES ALLEY

In addition to hitting the regular overhead that is taken before hitting the ground, you should practice smashing lobs after letting them bounce once. In this drill, the lobber stands behind the doubles alley and lobs balls very high toward the same alley across the net (Fig. 58.1). The drill is performed in the doubles alley since this provides a small and challenging target.

Fig. 58.1 Practice smashing the bouncing lob into doubles alley.

SMASH BOUNCING LOBS TOWARD SIDES OF COURT

In this drill, the lobber stands behind the right half of his singles court just behind the baseline, while you, standing in your forecourt, smash the lobs toward him for a few minutes (Fig. 58.2). Repeat this drill with the lobber standing behind the left half of his singles court.

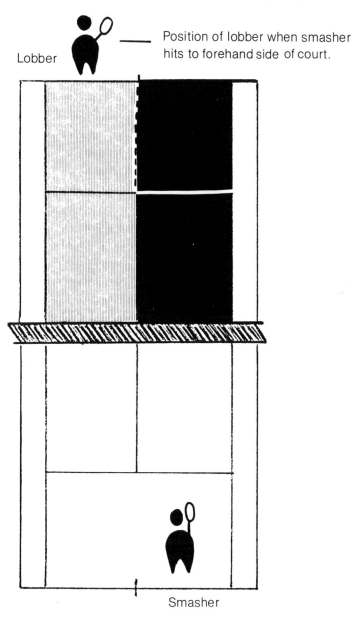

Fig. 58.2 Smashing lobs, after they bounce, toward forehand and backhand sides of singles court.

Lobber

Position of lobber when smasher hits to forehand side of court.

Smasher

Drill **59**

SMASH-TO-SIDELINE DRILL

Advanced or tournament players must aim overheads closer to the sideline than intermediates. In this drill a rally is developed by one player lobbing and the other smashing the lob before it bounces.

The smasher aims the overhead four feet from either singles sideline (Fig. 59). By directing the overhead four feet from the sideline, we can often move the ball out of an opponent's reach, and yet maintain a four-foot safety margin.

When we hit the short smashes that land near the sideline and close to the net, we create greater angles for more outright winners. Deep overheads that land near the baseline are less risky for the smasher, but are often returnable. Use more racket head speed when standing between the service line and the net than when smashing in the backcourt area. As in Fig. 58.2, the smasher aims overheads to one side for a few minutes, then switches to the other sideline target.

Fig. 59   Smash-to-sideline drill.

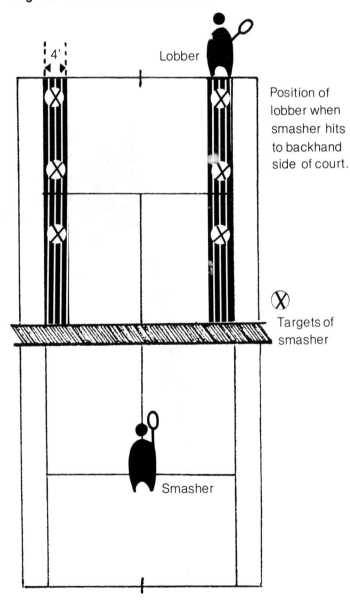

Lobber

Position of lobber when smasher hits to backhand side of court.

Targets of smasher

Smasher

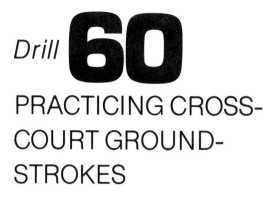

Drill 60

PRACTICING CROSS-COURT GROUND-STROKES

Crosscourt shots have greater accuracy potential than those aimed down the line because of the lower net in the middle, and the longer diagonal hitting area. Continually attempt to increase pace without sacrificing too much control. If you are hitting balls which land more than six feet beyond the boundary lines or strike the bottom of the net, you are probably swinging too hard. On groundstrokes take the ball early or at waist height in order to develop an offensive game.

CROSSCOURT FOREHAND DRILL

Two players rally crosscourt using forehands, hitting either deep into the baseline corner, or short and close to the singles sideline (Figs. 60.1A and B). The latter sharply angled shot forces your partner further out of court. However, direct most balls between your partner's service line and baseline.

When your partner hits short (inside the service line without a good angle) take advantage and come to the net and volley one or two balls back to him crosscourt. Without breaking the rally, retreat to your original position three feet behind the baseline and continue the exchange. Use mainly crosscourt drives, but try a few slices, especially when approaching the net.

After stroking a forehand shot from your baseline corner, move toward the center of the court behind the baseline to guarantee that you receive shots on the forehand side. This is also good movement practice. Do not allow balls to bounce a second time, and play balls landing outside the court area with as much effort as those which land in the singles court. If you wish you can place your racket covers on the court as targets.

Fig. 60.1 Crosscourt forehand drill.

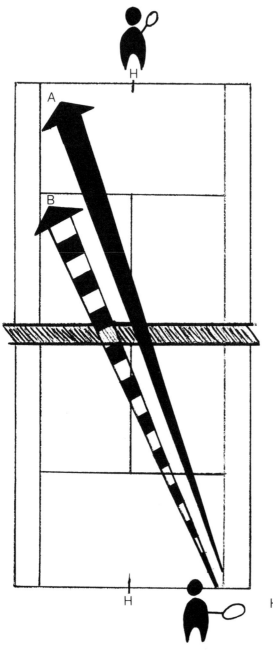

A = Target for
     deep forehand.

B = Target for
     short-angled
     forehand.

H = Home base area
     that players return
     to between hitting
     crosscourt forehands.

60.1A

148

60.1B

This is the same as the crosscourt forehand drill, except that the backhand slice is recommended as the primary shot instead of the drive since it is usually more accurate (Figs. 60.2A and B).

Fig. 60.2 Crosscourt backhand drill.

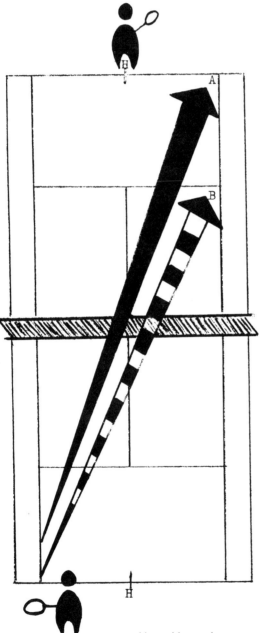

A = Target for deep backhand.

B = Target for short-angled backhand.

H = Home base area that players return to between hitting crosscourt backhands.

60.2A

60.2B   Stroking a backhand approach shot off a short ball.

Drill 61

PRACTICING DOWN-THE-LINE GROUNDSTROKES

DOWN-THE-LINE GROUNDSTROKES IN SINGLES COURT

Two players standing on opposite baselines rally the ball near and parallel to the singles sideline. One player strokes forehands and the other backhands, attempting deep shots (Fig. 61.1). Aim three or four feet from the sideline and close to the baseline. After a few minutes the partners reverse roles—the forehand hitter stroking backhands and the backhand hitter stroking forehands.

When your partner hits short, come to the net with an approach shot directed down the line to your partner, and volley one or two balls before returning to the baseline to continue the exchange. As in the previous drill, after stroking a ball from the baseline corner, move toward the center of the court behind the baseline.

DOWN-THE-LINE GROUNDSTROKES IN DOUBLES ALLEY

A simple yet effective drill is to stroke down the line into the doubles alley. In this drill the players have the option of working on either the forehand or backhand groundstroke and are challenged by the small, clearly marked target (Fig. 61.2).

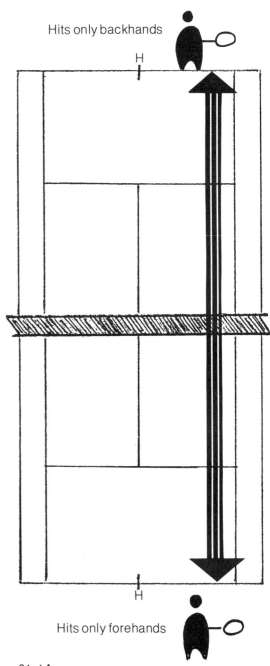

Fig. 61.1 Practicing down-the-line groundstrokes in the singles court.

Hits only backhands

Hits only forehands

61.1A

Fig. 61.2   Groundstroke drilling in doubles alley.

Players can either use the forehand or backhand groundstroke.

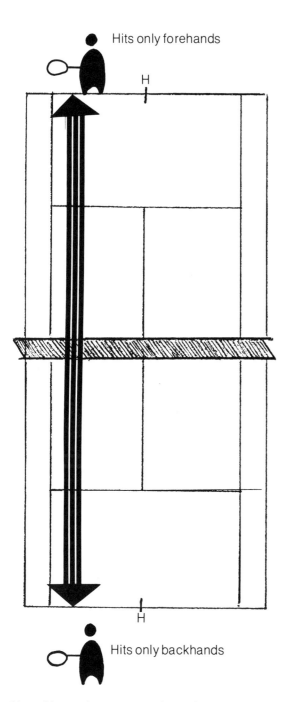

Hits only forehands

H

Hits only backhands

H = Home base area that players return to after hitting down-the-line shot from near the sideline.

61.1B

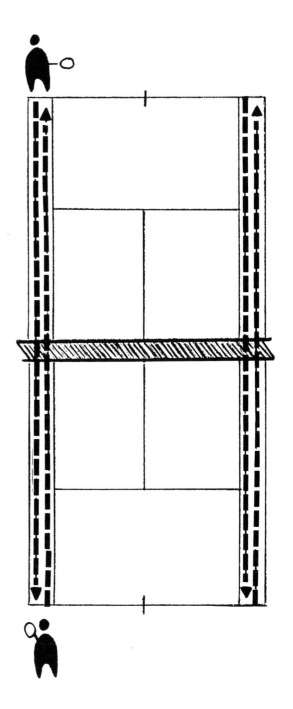

62

GROUNDSTROKE DRILL TO WEAK PLAYER'S BEST STROKE

This drill is used when one player's ability is far superior to another. The better player is in the back of the court aiming all groundstrokes to the weaker player's best stroke, usually the forehand. The less-skilled player moves the better player around, hitting anyplace in the singles court (Fig. 62). If the weaker partner hits short, the stronger player should approach the net and volley one or two balls to the weaker player's best stroke.

Both players benefit by practicing in this manner. The drill is an excellent conditioner for the better player who is forced to move around by his partner's unpredictable placement.

The stronger player should hit against the wind. If the wind has considerable velocity it can almost equalize ability.

Fig. 62 Groundstroke drill to weaker player's forehand.

Weaker Player Always stands in corner of his strongest side and tries to hit the ball away from his more skilled partner.

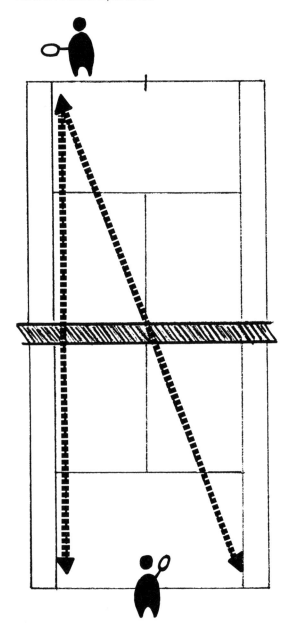

Stronger Player Directs all of his shots toward weaker player's best stroke.

Drill **63**

HALF-VOLLEY RALLYING WITH PARTNER

If you volley in matches, you will be forced to half-volley occasionally. With you and your partner standing in opposite courts between the service line and the net, establish a half-volley rally (Fig. 63). Use either forehand or backhand, and take each ball as soon as it starts to rise from the bounce.

Fig. 63 Half-volley rallying with partner. Take each ball immediately after it hits the ground.

Drill **64**

CLOSE-VOLLEYING

Close-volleying forces a player to take a short backswing, and to switch grips fast if using the two-grip method. You and a partner stand a yard inside the service line on opposite courts, and rally the ball back and forth without allowing it to touch the ground (Fig. 64). Hit firmly and keep the ball low. Do not overspin the volley, and meet the ball well in front of you.

CLOSE-VOLLEYING IN NON-TENNIS AREA

If a court is unavailable this drill can be easily done in an enclosed area such as a playground or a fenced basketball court. A fence eliminates the necessity of chasing distant balls. The drill can even be done in a grass field. In these instances it is advisable to tie a piece of string or cord between two objects, and place newspapers over the cord to resemble a net.

CLOSE-VOLLEYING IN HOME OR OFFICE

If you have a partner and a large living room, playroom, or office, you can participate in a volley "feel" drill. Standing six feet from your partner and facing him, softly volley a ball back and forth off the forehand without allowing it to bounce.

In order that a rally be easily maintained, arch the ball two feet above the racket. After two or three minutes, switch and start backhand-to-backhand close volleying.

Fig. 64   Close-volleying. Do not allow the ball to bounce.

Drill **65**

VOLLEY FOOTWORK DRILLS

Fig. 65.1 Backcourt volley footwork drill. Keep feet moving throughout this drill; make sure you step in the direction you are volleying.

BACKCOURT VOLLEY FOOTWORK DRILL

Standing two yards behind the service line, your partner in the same place in the opposite court, volley the ball back and forth without allowing it to hit the ground (Fig. 65.1). On each volley make sure you step toward your partner with the proper foot. Practicing backcourt volleys allows you sufficient time to utilize correct footwork.

VOLLEY FOOTWORK WITH GROUNDSTROKES

In this drill you are going to practice your volley from the service line, where volleying is more difficult than close to the net. You will develop the ability to advance closer to the net in order to gain a better volleying position.

To start the drill, stand two yards behind your service line, while a partner stands slightly behind his baseline in the opposite court. A rally is established as the partner groundstrokes a ball that you step forward to volley at the service line. You will then quickly retreat two or three steps as the ball is going back to him, and then come forward for the next volley (Fig. 65.2).

Fig. 65.2   Volley footwork drill.

Court position for volley footwork drill with partner at baseline.

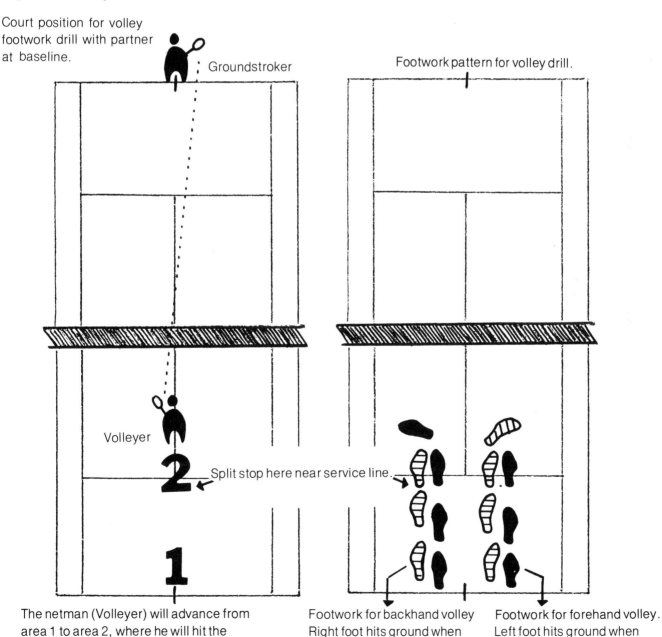

Groundstroker

Footwork pattern for volley drill.

Volleyer

2

Split stop here near service line.

1

The netman (Volleyer) will advance from area 1 to area 2, where he will hit the volley. He then retreats to area 1.

Footwork for backhand volley. Right foot hits ground when racket meets ball.

Footwork for forehand volley. Left foot hits ground when racket meets ball.

Your advance to the net begins as the ball is approaching the groundstroker. Take two quick steps and split stop as your partner groundstrokes the ball. After the split stop, if the ball comes to your backhand, step forward with your right foot as you volley the ball. If the ball comes to your forehand step forward with your left foot as you volley the ball. The volleyer has to move very quickly in order to execute this drill properly.

VOLLEY FOOTWORK DRILL ON BACKBOARD

When a court or adequate partner is unavailable, the backboard is an excellent means to improve volley footwork. In this volley footwork drill you will be as active as possible with your feet.

In order to have the time to do this drill properly, stand at least fifteen feet from the backboard, and volley toward a target located six to seven feet from the ground (Fig. 65.3). This allows you ample time to step toward the wall with your right foot on the backhand volley and left on the forehand volley. Keep a rally going as long as possible, concentrating on the correct footwork.

Fig. 65.3 Volley footwork drill at backboard. Keep your feet moving in this exercise.

Drill **66**

TOUCH-VOLLEY DRILLS

TOUCH-VOLLEY DRILL ON BACKBOARD

The touch or stop volley can be a great weapon if executed properly. It can easily be developed on a backboard. Standing six feet from the wall, volley three balls at normal speed, then touch-volley the fourth ball into a target located just above a three-foot net-line mark (Fig. 66.1). (Therefore you cadence will be "one, two, three, touch," "one, two, three, touch," etc.) Have your weight going toward the wall as you prepare to contact the ball. However, stop forward movement of the racket at impact by blocking the ball with the racket. This will take all speed off the ball. Do thirty stop volleys using both forehand and backhand.

Fig. 66.1 Touch-volley drill on backboard. Keep the stop-volley as soft and as low over the netline as possible.

TOUCH-VOLLEY DRILL ON COURT

With your partner standing on the opposite baseline, and you positioned ten feet from the net, he ground-strokes balls which you touch-volley (Fig. 66.2). A good touch volley must pass low over the net (within a foot and a half) and land close to the net so your opponent will not have time to reach it. Hold the racket loosely as you make a stop volley.

Fig. 66.2 Touch-volley drill on court.

Drill 67

LOB-VOLLEY DRILLS

LOB-VOLLEY DRILL ON BACKBOARD

The lob volley is used in advanced doubles, and occasionally in singles, by tournament-level players. Standing seven feet from the backboard, hit three volleys at normal speed, then lob the next volley nine or ten feet high (Fig. 67.1). (Your cadence will be ''one, two, three, lob,'' ''one, two, three, lob,'' etc.) Practice fifteen lob volleys on both forehand and backhand.

Fig. 67.1   Lob-volley drill on backboard.

LOB-VOLLEY DRILL ON COURT

This drill is performed with two players standing a yard inside their service lines with a large number of balls available. They close-volley back and forth, then one player lob-volleys just above and beyond the reach of his partner (Fig. 67.2). Hit fifteen lob volleys on both forehand and backhand, and then partners switch roles.

Fig. 67.2 Lob-volley drill on court.

Drill **68**

VOLLEY TO UTILIZE MAXIMUM RACKET LENGTH

When moving to intercept a passing shot close to the net, every extra inch you can reach becomes vital. Sometimes when extremely close to the net, the mere act of touching the ball with the racket can produce an outright winner. The following technique increases your reach by four inches in executing a stab volley.

Grasp the racket at the very end of the handle with the index and middle fingers and the thumb (Fig. 68.1). Using this emergency grip, and extending your racket reach to the side as far as possible, start a volley rally on a backboard (Fig. 68.2). Do this exercise for a few minutes. Then, using your regular grip, volley three or four balls and direct the next ball wide, forcing you to extend your reach and to stab-volley. On the wide ball, make the quick change to your stab-volley grip. Do these exercises on the backhand as well as the forehand side.

Fig. 68.1 Emergency grip to maximize volley reach.

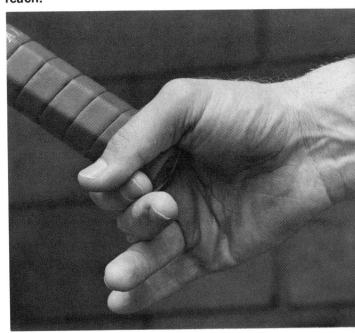

Fig. 68.2   Stab-volleying with emergency grip.

Drill 69

VOLLEY RALLYING AND ADVANCING TOWARD NET

If a player wishes to be in the close-to-the-net position where he can put a volley away, he should practice moving toward the net.

Standing slightly inside your baselines on opposite sides of the court, you and a partner advance to the net while you volley back and forth. When you reach a point ten feet from the net, stop advancing but continue volleying until the ball is missed. Then return to your baseline and start the rally again (Fig. 69).

Fig. 69   Volley rally and advancing toward net.

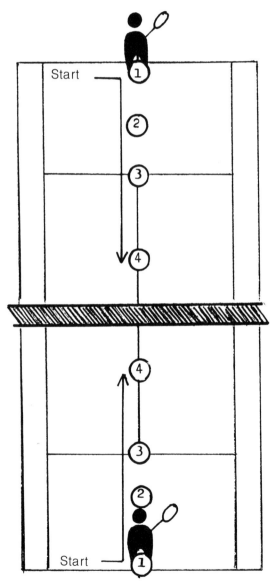

1 Volley rally starts here and players hit one volley and then advance to area 2.

2 Players hit one volley and then advance to area 3.

3 Players volley once and advance to area 4.

4 Players stop here and close-volley until someone misses. Then they return to the starting position (1) and begin a new volley rally.

Drill **70**

QUICK VOLLEY DRILL

This drill improves the racket quickness of the volleyer, and gives him confidence and courage to react fast when an overhead is directed at him. The smasher begins this exercise by standing a foot behind the baseline of the doubles alley. He tosses a ball in the air, allows it to bounce, then smashes it directly at his partner who is in the same alley across the net. The volleyer must stand and remain between the net and an imaginary extension of the service line. The overhead is volleyed back to the smasher in the doubles alley. There are no rallies (Fig. 70).

After the player has good timing on his volley, the smasher then moves up the alley to a point nine feet inside the baseline and hits overheads from there. If the smasher does not have a powerful overhead he can move even closer to the net.

For obvious reasons, variations of this drill are called "suicide" or "the cage." The latter term refers to the fact that the volleyer must remain in a confined area.

Fig. 70 Quick volley drill. Smasher first takes position 1, then 2. Position 3 is only used if the smasher lacks power. Volleyer must remain inside striped area and volleys the smash into the alley on the other side of the net. In this drill, the volleyer blocks all overheads back to smasher.

Drill 71

DRIVE, VOLLEY, LOB, AND OVERHEAD DRILL

This is, possibly, the most important tennis drill—it develops a variety of shots. With many balls available, one of the players stands on his service line while another stands just behind the baseline of the opposite court. A rally is established with the baseliner either driving or lobbing the ball, while the netman volleys or smashes back to the baseliner, depending upon the kind of shot given. There is no set stroke order for this drill (Fig. 71).

BASELINER'S INTENT—DRIVES

The baseliner's shots should pass low over the net (within one and a half feet), with topspin on the forehand and with topspin or slice on the backhand. All shots should be hit with pace except for the slow dink which is an effective backhand slice shot. He should aim the balls within reach of the volleyer so that a rally can be maintained.

BASELINER'S INTENT—LOBS

The baseliner's offensive lobs should be disguised. They are usually aimed at the netman's backhand side. Offensive lobs should be directed deep to one corner or the other. He should use the offensive lob whenever he sees his partner close to the net. In this drill, you should lob once every four or five shots or more. Occasionally a topspin forehand lob should be attempted. Offensive lobs should generally be hit when the lobber is inside his baseline.

The defensive lob should only be used when the lobber is well behind his baseline. It should be hit extremely high and deep down the middle of the court.

NETMAN'S INTENT

In this drill, the netman's volleys should land between the service and baseline. He should learn to anticipate shots by observing the baseliner's body and racket positions just before ball contact is made. He should perfect his anticipation to the point that he almost always gets his racket on an offensive lob. His volleys should be hard enough so that his partner has difficulty making a good offensive lob or a low screaming drive.

Fig. 71   Drive, volley, lob, and overhead drill.

Baseliner   Lobs anyplace in the court but aims drives or slices within netman's reach.

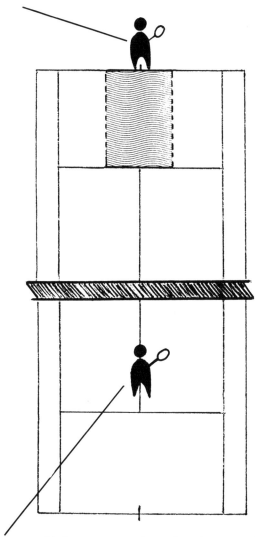

Netman   Volleys or smashes directly toward target. The netman tries to volley as deep as possible into the target area.

Drill **72**

PASSING SHOT AND CONDITIONING DRILL

This drill is popular among some of the world's leading players and involves a volleyer and a groundstroker. The volleyer stands in a service box and volleys within his partner's reach, forcing him to run as much as possible. After an error stops the rally, another ball is immediately put in play. Fifteen or twenty balls should be used.

The groundstroker takes the balls after the first bounce and returns them hard and low to the netman. If the drill is performed vigorously, the groundstroker will tire in about five or ten minutes, and will then switch places with the netman (Fig. 72).

Fig. 72   Passing shot and conditioning drill.

Groundstroker   Hits balls directly back to volleyer.

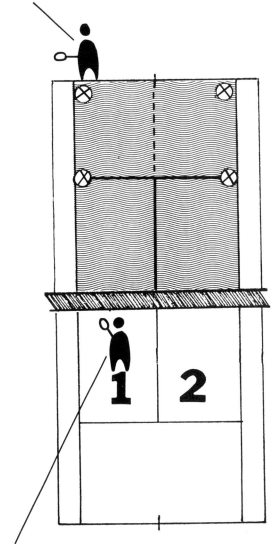

Volleyer   Stands at either point 1 or 2 and moves partner by hitting (not too hard) to one of the target areas (⊗).

Drill **73**

THREE-PLAYER DRILLS

These drills are designed for three players, with two players on one side of the net and one player on the other. The lone player receives the drill focus and derives the most benefit. Some of these drills were popularized by Australian Davis Cup teams.

TWO AT NET AND ONE AT BASELINE

Balls directed at baseliner: Two players, standing on the same side of the court and in adjoining service boxes, hit volleys or overheads in the vicinity of the baseliner. The baseliner strokes either passing shots or lobs to alternate corners of the singles court, like in a match. A rally is sustained as long as possible. The baseliner can position himself at the center mark (Fig. 73.1A) or in one of the baseline corners (Fig. 73.1B).

Balls directed away from baseliner (Fig. 73.1C): The netmen, with at least twenty balls available, aim all balls away from and barely within the reach of the groundstroker. After one ball is missed, another one is immediately put in play. If the drill is executed correctly, five minutes is the maximum time a player can withstand the running in this drill. He should be short of wind from continually running around the court.

Fig. 73.1 Two at net and one at baseline.

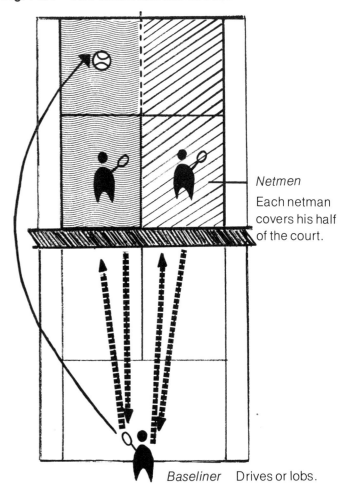

Netmen
Each netman covers his half of the court.

Baseliner Drives or lobs.

73.1A Volleys and overheads are aimed to baseliner who stands at center mark.

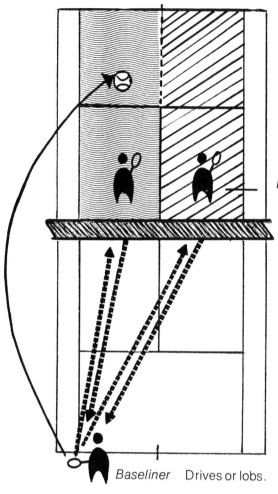

Netmen Each netman
covers his half of the court.

Baseliner Drives or lobs.

73.1B Volleys and overheads are aimed
to baseliner who stands in backhand corner.

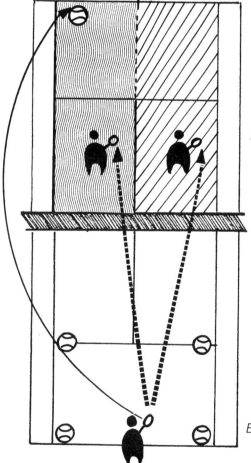

Netmen Place balls in
target areas ( ) and
barely within
reach of baseliner.

Baseliner Drives or lobs.
After five minutes players
rotate positions.

73.1C Volleys and overheads are
directed away from baseliner.

TWO AT BASELINE AND ONE AT NET

The netman, standing on the service line, hits alternately to baseliners in the opposite court (Fig. 73.2). The baseliners either drive to the netman or lob to him offensively or defensively. The drives are kept within the reach of the netman, but the offensive lobs are intended to land over his head in the corners of the singles court. The netman should aim for short-angled crosscourt volleys, as well as deep down-the-line volleys. He also angles overheads. The ground-strokers are responsible for reaching any kind of volley (even a touch volley) or overhead which hits on their half of the singles court.

Fig. 73.2   Two at baseline and one at net.

Baseliners   Either drive to netman or lob offensively away from him.

Netman   Hits volleys or overheads either deep to corners or short near sidelines.

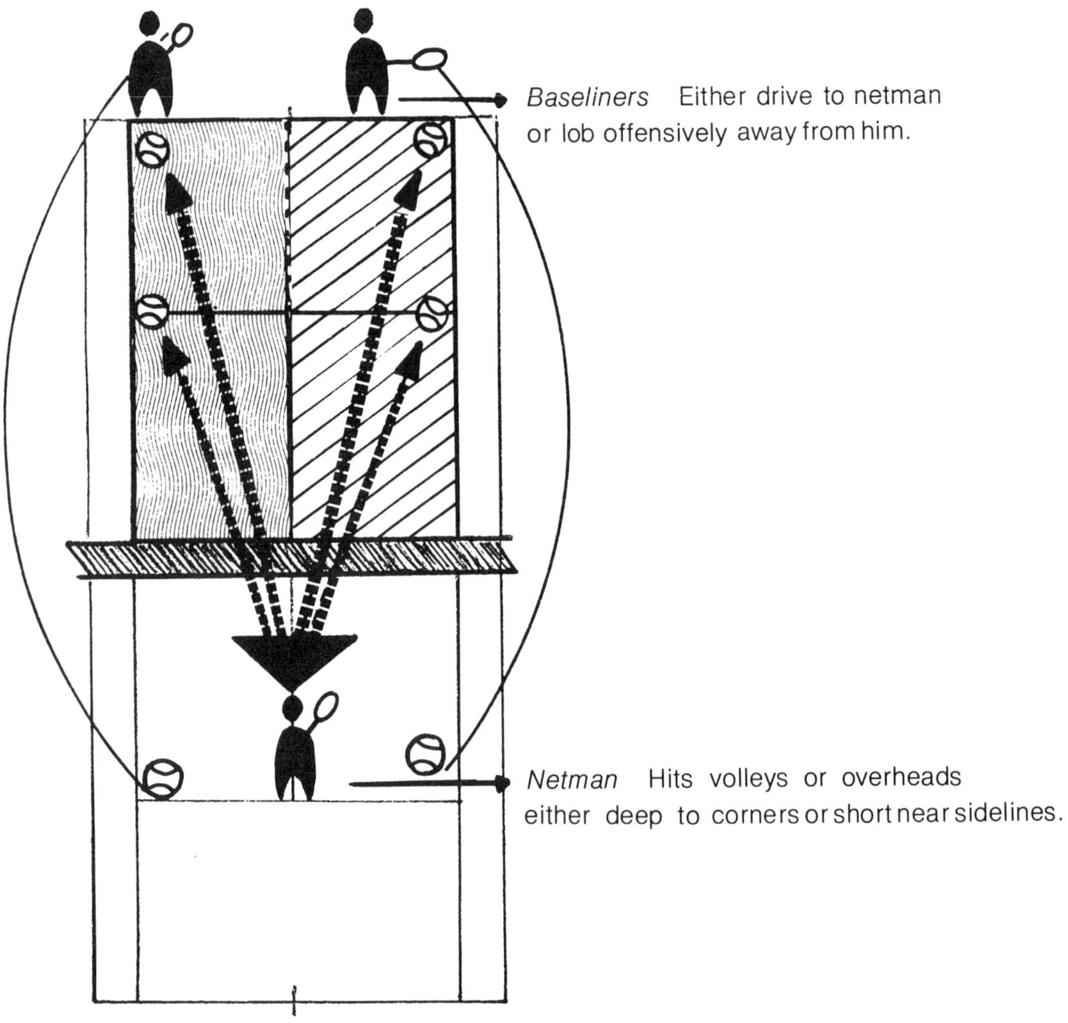

TWO PLAYERS ON ONE BASELINE AND THE THIRD ON THE OTHER

The solo baseliner alternates drives to both sides of the court. The two baseliners either aim balls directly at the solo player (Fig. 73.3A) or run him from corner to corner with drives or slices (Fig. 73.3B). The lone baseliner either strokes deep into the corners or attempts short angled drives.

Fig. 73.3 Two players on one baseline and a third on the other.

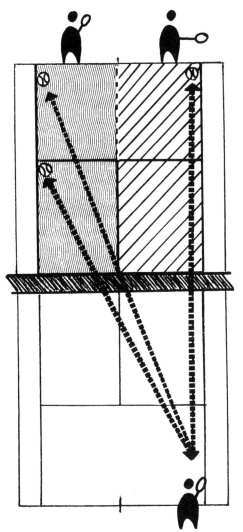

73.3A The two baseliners stroke directly at the opposite baseliner who is either in the forehand or backhand corner. All players use drives, slices, or loops.

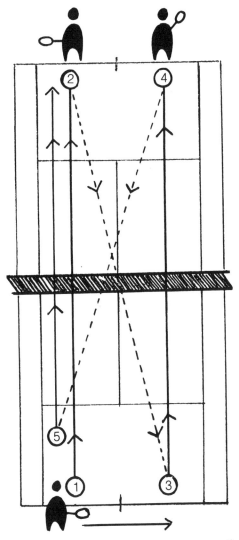

73.3B The two baseliners move their partner and keep the ball barely within his reach.

THREE-PLAYER CLOSE-VOLLEYING

Two players stand inside their service boxes on one side of the net, while a third player stands facing them on the center service line. A volley rally is established and maintained as long as possible (Fig. 73.4). The player who is hitting alone has the advantage of angling his volleys. High balls should be volleyed harder than low balls. Volleys should be sliced or hit flat (no overspin regardless of their height), and a short backswing should be used. The solo player can try to pass his partners within the boundaries of the singles court.

Fig. 73.4   Three-player close-volleying.

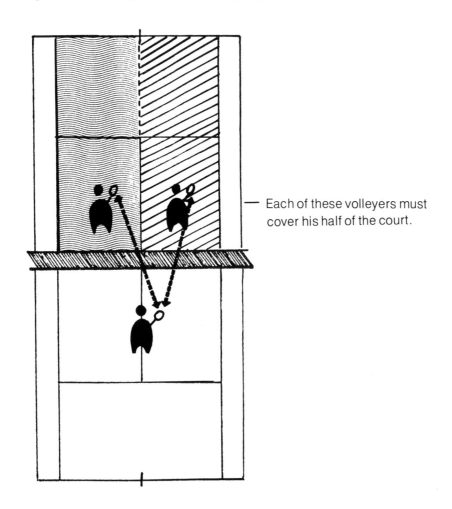

Each of these volleyers must cover his half of the court.

THREE-PLAYER DOUBLES DRILL

Regular doubles are vigorously played with the server and his netman on one side and a receiver playing half the court on the other side of the net. The serving team must keep all balls on one side of the receiver's court, while the receiver hits anyplace on their side. The center service line (and an imaginary extension of it) is a boundary line for the solo player. Ten-point games are played. The receiver can take the net, lob, or drive, as he would in a match. The server should try to get to the net. The receiver should play a game from the deuce court and then switch to the ad court (Fig. 73.5). Players rotate positions.

Fig. 73.5   Three-player doubles drill.

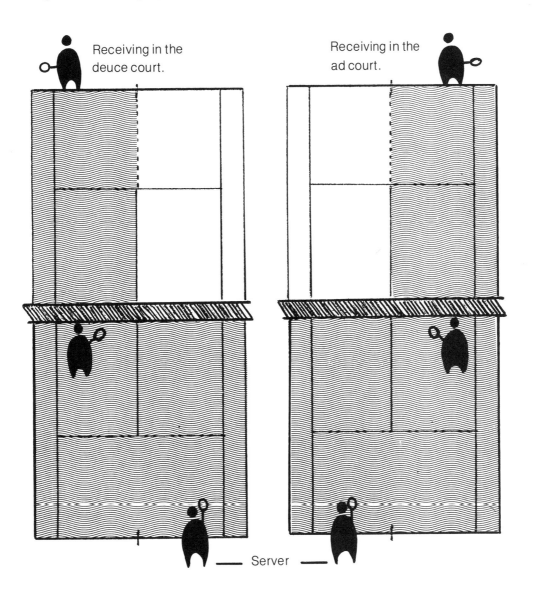

Receiving in the deuce court.

Receiving in the ad court.

—— Server ——

Drill 74

SERVING DRILLS

to occur as far away from the service box as possible. A good international-class second service hit by a man lands at least three feet up the fence after landing in the service box (the ball does not bounce on the ground after it lands in the service box) (Fig. 74.1).

DEVELOPING AN ADVANCED SECOND SERVICE

The second serve should be developed before the first service since an error on the second serve will result in an outright loss of a point. Accuracy should be developed before power.

The racket swing of the second serve should be just as fast as the first. Control is gained on the second service by placing spin on the ball. Make sure your weight is going in the same direction as your serve.

With a large number of balls on hand, start practicing your second service by aiming toward a service box on the court. To avoid shoulder injury, take numerous slow warm-up serves before swinging hard. Count the number of your consecutive good serves. Keep practicing until you can serve thirteen to fifteen in a row.

Set a small target. After you gain control of your second service, place one-square-yard targets at the corners of the deuce court. You can aim at bicycle tires, newspapers, or soda cans. Some players prefer to make mental targets. See how many second serves land in the target area in twenty attempts. Practice in the ad court as well as the deuce court. Do not be discouraged—hitting the target area is very difficult.

DEVELOPING AN ADVANCED FIRST SERVICE

The first service, if powerful, is the most important stroke in tennis because it can easily extract an error or a short, weak return. Continually attempt to add power to your first service. Think of accelerating *after* ball contact is made. Use the wrist as one of your key sources of power. When practicing the first service, aim close to the lines.

GAUGING SERVICE POWER

One method of checking your service power (and depth) is to watch where the ball hits the ground after it lands in the service box. Try to get this second bounce

Fig. 74.1 Gauging second service power.

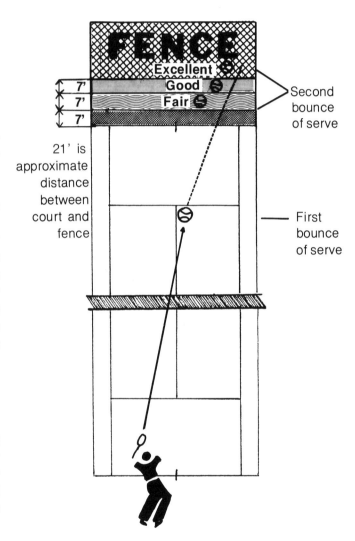

COMBINING FIRST AND SECOND SERVES

Practice your first service, and when you miss, use your second service. Try to keep your percentage of good first serves to fifty per cent or more. Vary the types of serves you use (flat, slice, or overspin) as well as placement.

Occasionally, have a player return your serves. This practice makes you concentrate on serving closer to the lines. When the receiver is forced to make a defensive return because of a wide serve, immediate and dramatic feedback of the effect of a well-placed serve is given the server (Fig. 74.2).

Fig. 74.2 Practicing serves with partner returning. Force receiver to stretch sideways when returning your first service. An apron used to store balls can be a time saver.

SERVING AND RUNNING TO NET

Advance to the net as quickly as possible after serving. Serve, sprint toward the net, and do a split stop on the service line (Fig. 74.3). See if you can land on the service line by the time your serve hits the fence. Practice this drill using first and second serves. Serve into the deuce and ad courts, from the doubles as well as the singles positions.

Do not foot-fault. Make sure your foot is not touching the baseline or the court as you strike the ball. Have your partner check for a foot fault (Fig. 74.4).

Fig. 74.4 Correcting a foot-fault condition. Place the racket handle on baseline throughout serve to prevent server from stepping on line.

Fig. 74.3 Serving and running to net.

Practice your service from the singles (S) and doubles (D) positions, and quickly advance to the split-stop position (X).

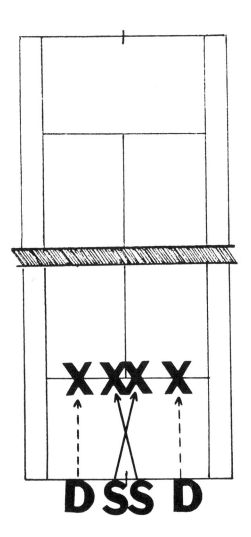

Drill **75**

SERVING UNDERHAND
WITH SPIN

The underhand serve with spin is an effective change of pace. It is especially good to use serving against the wind and in doubles. If a player has a sore shoulder he can allow it to recover by using an underhand service when playing games.

In order to be successful the serve must be delivered quickly, stay low, and land close to the net (Fig. 75.1). This serve, in reality, is a dropshot. The player should follow his serve into the net, since the return of service can easily be volleyed for a winner (providing you can get your racket on his return of service). The Continental grip should be used. Do not serve more than 100 balls at a session since the underhand service can strain the wrist (Figs.75.2A–D).

Fig. 75.1   Serving underhand with spin.

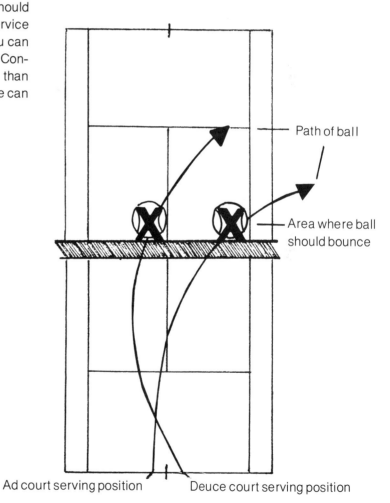

Path of ball

Area where ball should bounce

Ad court serving position   Deuce court serving position

Fig. 75.2   Serving underhand with spin.

75.2A   Ready to serve. Make this position look as if you were going to execute a normal service.

75.2B   Bring the racket back and make a short and low service toss.

75.2C   Undercut the ball with slice. The lower edge of the racket should be leading.

75.2D   Follow-through on underhand service.

Drill 76

RETURN-OF-SERVICE DRILL

A good return of service can often equalize a powerful service. It is consistent, yet flexible, varying with the type of service received. This drill, which includes service as well as return of service practice, is an excellent way to end workouts. Although the drill is valuable on courts of medium speed, it is doubly worthwhile on fast surfaces offering a greater challenge to the returner.

When receiving service you should have your weight going toward the direction of the service return. If you carefully watch the server's ball toss, timing of the return can be improved and the type of service often anticipated. In addition, watch the ball closely as it comes to you. When returning very powerful serves, use a short backswing and think of the return like a volley.

POSITION OF RECEIVER

Return service by standing in one of three areas (Fig. 76). The first (position 1) is on the baseline near the singles sideline. The second (2) is halfway between the service line and baseline, where a very weak service or a high bouncing twist should be returned. The third (3) is about six feet behind the baseline where a very hard serve is more easily returned. The receiver's position should bisect the angle of probable service direction.

DIRECTION OF SERVICE RETURNS

In this return-of-service drill, the server places his serves to one spot, the backhand or forehand corner of either service box. He hammers away at that same corner for fifteen or twenty serves, then directs them to another target.

The returner aims balls to one of four places (Fig. 76). Two of the service return targets (A and B) are located in the backcourt, where it is effective to place the ball against an opponent who serves and stays in the back of the court. Two other targets (C and D) are placed on the service lines, near the sidelines, to cope with the player who follows his serve to net. When using the latter targets keep the return of service low. No points are played out in this drill.

Fig. 76   Return-of-service drill.

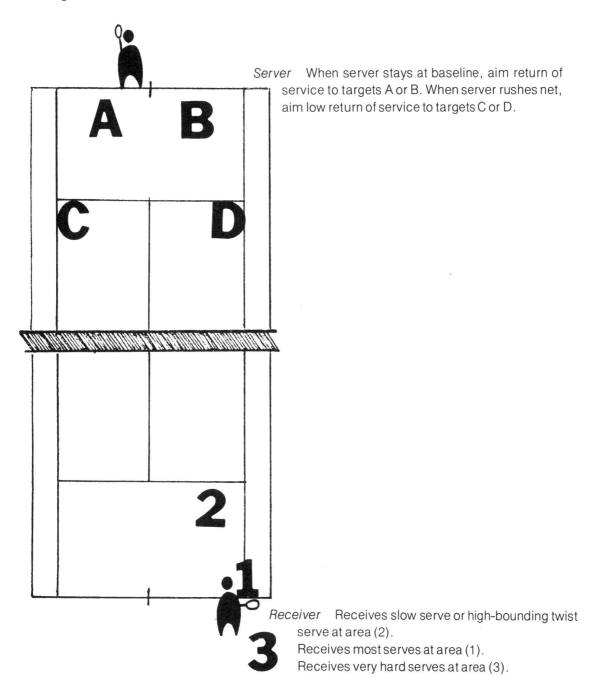

Server   When server stays at baseline, aim return of service to targets A or B. When server rushes net, aim low return of service to targets C or D.

Receiver   Receives slow serve or high-bounding twist serve at area (2).
Receives most serves at area (1).
Receives very hard serves at area (3).

TOPSPIN GROUND-STROKE PRACTICE

Developing overspin on groundstrokes is very important to the hardhitting tournament player because it is the method by which he can control his powerful shots. Since topspin makes the ball bounce forward, the hitter receives a bonus of extra length. Overspin also brings the ball down, and as a result the low ball is difficult for the net rusher to volley.

To get pronounced topspin, slightly exaggerate your normal drives so that the racket follows a more severe low-to-high direction. Think of the strings as grabbing the back of the ball and temporarily holding it. Make sure the racket head is flat or slightly closed at point of contact (Figs. 77.1A–C) and in the follow-through. Try to finish the stroke with the head of your racket above the top of your own head.

Fig. 77.1   Racket face positions at ball contact.

77.1A   Flat racket face. Racket head is perpendicular to ground.

77.1B   Closed racket face. Top edge of racket head is nearest the net and leads the stroke.

77.1C   Open racket face. Bottom edge of racket head is closest to net and leads the stroke. The open racket face is used only when slicing; it is not used for topspin or flat shots.

In this drill, your partner is at the net in the opposite court, while you are behind your baseline. The partner volleys the ball, and you return it with topspin off either the forehand or backhand to establish a rally (Fig. 77.2). If a partner is unavailable, you can practice your overspin groundstrokes on a backboard.

Fig. 77.2   Topspin backhand follow-through.

Drill **78**

DROPSHOT DRILL

The drop shot is intended to win points as well as tire opponents. On clay courts it is often used to bring a weak volleyer to the net. The drop shot is aimed low over the net and drops close to the net and near the sideline. Use a slice action. Almost always execute the drop shot from inside your baseline. (As a supplement to the following exercises, Drill 91 is excellent for developing the drop shot in a game situation.)

DROPSHOT PRACTICE WITH PARTNER AT NET

With a partner at the net and you just inside the opposite baseline, dropshot every ball that he volleys toward you, using either the forehand or backhand (Fig. 78.1). By having a partner at the net, you can practice the drop shot and maintain a rally. The volleyer gets practice in returning the dink, which is identical with the drop shot and used when an opponent is at the net. A dink from the backhand should be in the repertoire of every player.

Fig. 78.1 Dropshot practice with partner at net. Groundstroker hits slow drop shots (dinks) to volleyer.

DROP SHOT IN LONG-SHORT GROUNDSTROKE COMBINATIONS

The drop shot is best used when you have an opponent very deep behind the baseline. It is used preferably on one side of the court. If directed toward the backhand side it is especially effective. You and a partner rally a few deep crosscourt groundstrokes from opposite baselines, and you will then hit a drop shot down the line. The partner does not pursue the drop shot, and another rally begins. After a few minutes do this same drill from the other crosscourt position.

DROPSHOT PRACTICE ON A BACKBOARD

Dropshot ability can be developed on a backboard. Stand twenty or twenty-five feet from the wall and hit one or two hard drives, then dropshot to a target located within two feet above the net line.

Fig. 78.2 Drop shot after deep crosscourt exchange.

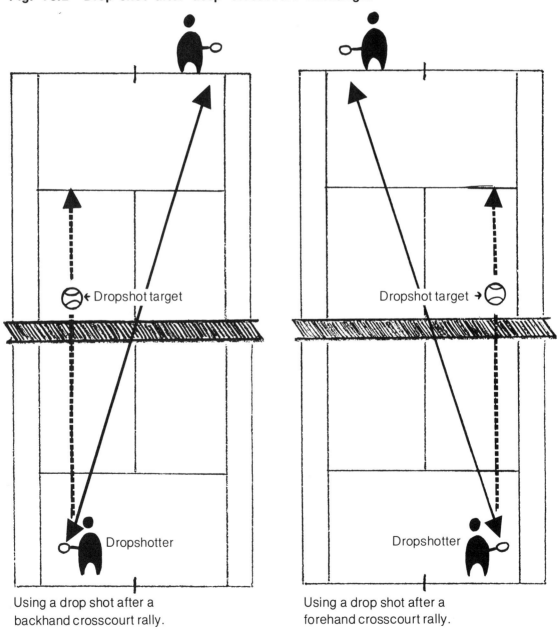

Using a drop shot after a
backhand crosscourt rally.

Using a drop shot after a
forehand crosscourt rally.

Drill 79

GROUNDSTROKE LOOPS

A tournament–clay-court player must know how to cope with loops or high-floating balls and should be able to hit them. To be on the receiving end of these shots is a shock to a person who has not experienced them, such as a California hard-court player. The loop is not effective in top tournament tennis on cement, asphalt, or even grass or wood surfaces. The loop is executed like a low offensive lob, and used when both players are in the backcourt area.

HITTING LOOPS

With you and a partner standing on opposite baselines, stroke down-the-line forehand and backhand loops and then crosscourt the loops. Try to put overspin on the forehand stroke so the ball will hop forward after the bounce. Hitting a topspin backhand loop is difficult, but possible. The loop should be aimed twelve to fifteen feet in the air.

RECEIVING LOOPS

When receiving loops, stand in one of three places. The first is inside the baseline, where you can take floaters on the rise. The second receiving position is a yard or two behind the baseline—stroke the loops near their peak. The third position is eight to twelve feet behind the baseline, where loops are hit after they come down from their high bounce (Fig. 79).

Fig. 79   Exchanging groundstroke loops.

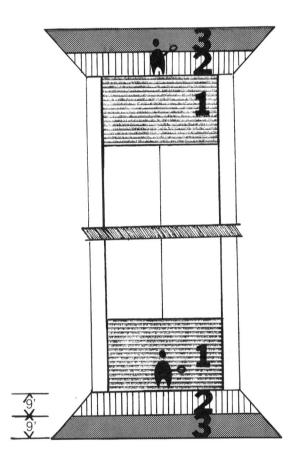

Receivers' Positions
1. Area for taking looped balls on the rise.
2. Area for taking looped balls near their peak.
3. Area for taking looped balls after they come down.

Drill **80**

TIE-BREAKER PRACTICE

If a player has had minimal experience with tie breakers, he should practice them separately from playing sets. Use the particular tie-break system that will be used in your forthcoming tournament or competitive matches. Tie breakers should be practiced until the player is fully confident of his ability to play them.

They are also excellent to use when two players do not have time to play a full set yet want to play points. You and your partner can play for a half-hour or hour keeping track of the number of tie breakers that each has won.

Drill # **81**

HALF-COURT DRILLS

These six drills are used by some of the world's greatest professionals. They are excellent because they promote long rallies while playing points. Although offensive shots occur in these drills, it is difficult to put the ball away. Crosscourt hitting is emphasized which benefits doubles as well as singles play.

In these drills the court is divided into halves, with the center service line and an imaginary extension of it to the baseline dividing the two parts. One doubles alley is included in each half of the court. The partners play points without keeping score.

HALF-COURT DRILLS FROM BASELINE

In these three drills you and a partner will stand at your baselines taking the ball after one bounce. Try to move each other as much as possible with a combination of drives, slices, and occasional loops. If you are drawn to the net for a drop shot, remain in the forecourt position and play the point out. Then return to the baseline to begin another point (Figs. 81.1A–C).

Fig. 81.1 Half-court drill with partners at baselines.

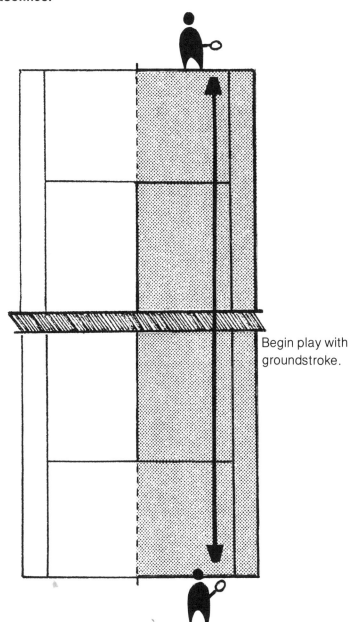

Begin play with groundstroke.

81.1A Playing baseline points down the line.

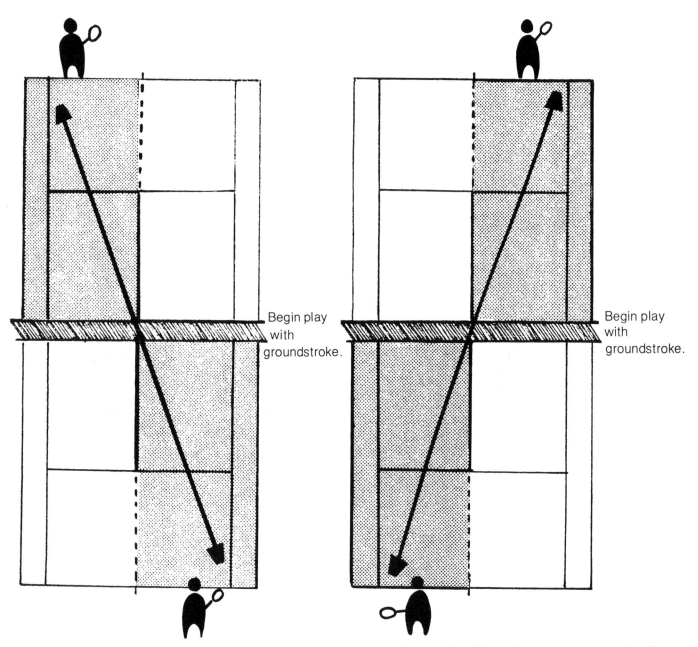

Begin play
with
groundstroke.

Begin play
with
groundstroke.

81.1B   Playing baseline points crosscourt,
primarily using forehands.

81.1C   Playing baseline points crosscourt, primarily
using backhands.

194

HALF-COURT DRILLS WITH NETMAN AND BASELINER

The baseliner takes the ball after the first bounce and lobs, passes, or hits slow dinks in an attempt to win the point. The netman, taking the ball before it bounces, tries to put the ball away or to extract an error from the baseliner by volleying or smashing. If the netman brings his partner to the forecourt with a drop volley, the two then volley the point out at close range (Figs. 81.2A–C).

Fig. 81.2 Half-court drill with one player at net and partner in backcourt.

Begin play with groundstroke.

81.2A   Playing down-the-line points.

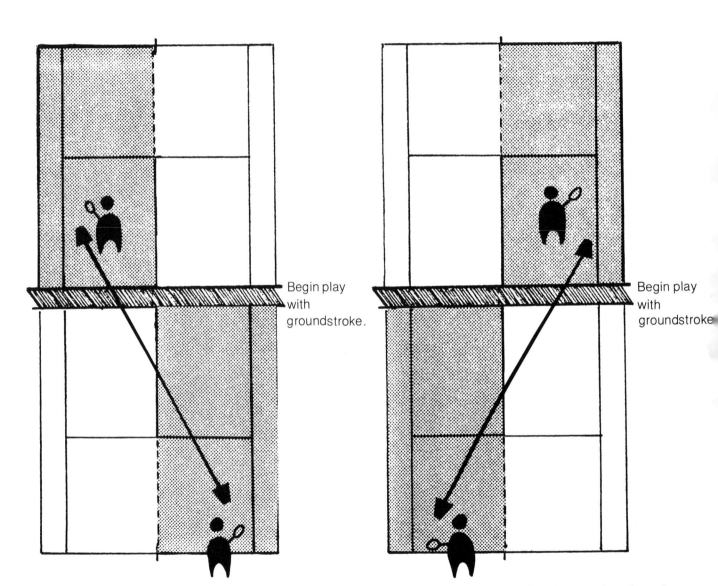

Begin play
with
groundstroke.

Begin play
with
groundstroke

81.2B Playing crosscourt points, primarily
using forehands.

81.2C Playing crosscourt points, primarily using
backhands.

Drill 82

DOWN-THE-LINE AND CROSSCOURT GROUND-STROKE DRILL

This drill accents stroking on the move while maintaining a rally. If you can stroke accurately when moving, you will not have to worry about hitting from a stationary position. This drill is very tiring so do not expect to do it more than a few minutes.

Standing at the baselines for drilling in the singles court, put a groundstroke in play down the line (parallel with sideline) while your partner from the other side of the net returns the ball crosscourt (diagonally). Take all balls after the first bounce and repeat the pattern of one player hitting all shots down the line and the other continually crosscourting (Fig. 82A). Maintain a rally as long as possible. After a ball is missed, another is immediately put in play.

Fig. 82 Down-the-line and crosscourt ground-stroke drill.

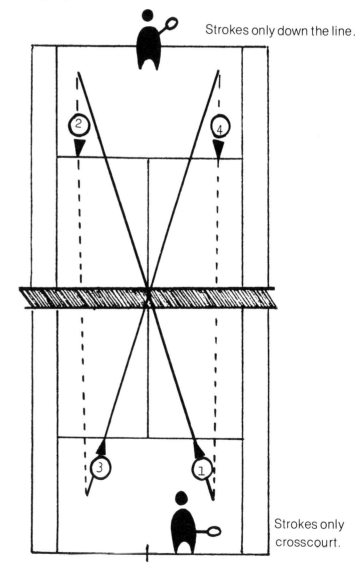

82A Drill with crosscourter stroking deep into corners.

197

After a few minutes switch roles—you hit crosscourt and your partner aims down the line. You might be asking yourself which of the two does the most running. If the crosscourter hits good short-angled shots that maneuver the partner outside of the singles sideline, then the down-the-liner will certainly have to run the most (Fig. 82B). The players should attempt to take the ball early in order to be more offensive.

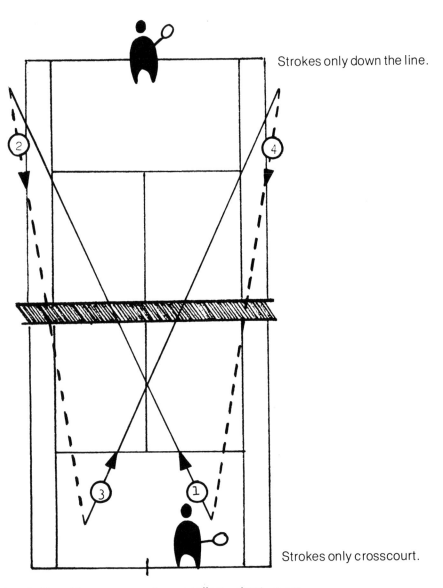

Strokes only down the line.

Strokes only crosscourt.

82B Drill with crosscourter angling short near sidelines. (Notice the greater distance the down-the-line hitter must run in 82B than 82A.)

Drill **83**

PASS-ME DRILL

This passing shot and lob drill teaches a baseliner to defend himself against the net rusher. The netman learns to improve anticipation. With one player at the net and the other at the baseline of the opposite court, the baseliner tries to: (1) pass the netman, (2) lob over his head, or (3) extract an error.

The netman directs all his volleys and smashes deep and down the middle, while the baseliner attempts to create an opening for a winning shot by driving, dinking, or lobbing. Although rallies develop, points are not counted (Fig. 83).

To be successful against a netman of tournament calibre, the baseliner should try to hit hard, low, and near the sidelines, with overspin. As a calculated risk, the baseliner should take the ball early in order to pass the netman. He should use the offensive lob frequently but with disguise, appearing until the last second as if he is going to hit a passing shot. The baseliner should vary the direction of his passing shots so the netman is unable to detect a pattern.

Fig. 83 Pass-me drill. Net person volleys or smashes deep down the middle. Baseliner tries to pass or lob the net person on every ball except the one he puts in play.

Drill **84**

CROSSCOURT ANGLE-
TOUCH DRILL

This drill is excellent to develop touch, dropshot ability, and mastery of crosscourt angle shots. Standing in the forehand service box, with a partner diagonally opposite, rally the ball as close to the net and the singles sideline as possible. Take all balls after the first bounce using only forehand drives and slices (Fig. 84.1). Do not keep score.

After rallying for two or three minutes from the forehand service boxes, move to the other service box and hit crosscourt backhands (Fig. 84.2). Use the slice on the backhand swing.

Fig. 84.1 Forehand crosscourt angle-touch drill. To improve speed afoot, players return to center service line after stroking the ball.

Fig. 84.2 Backhand crosscourt angle–touch drill. Players return to center service line after stroking the ball.

Drill **85**

CROSSCOURT ANGLE-VOLLEY DRILL

The angled volley is a put-away volley. This rare drill perfects sharply angled volleys and pays dividends in both singles and doubles play.

The players position themselves and conduct the drill exactly as the previous one, except they volley each ball instead of allowing it to bounce. Volleys should be soft and low to force players to bend. Volleyers should hit at such extreme crosscourt angles that they experience a feeling of hitting almost parallel with the net. Volley three to five minutes with the forehand, and then the backhand. Refer to the illustrations in Drill 84.

TEN-POINT GAME PROCEDURES FOR DRILLS 86–93

The last eight drills should be played on a competitive ten-point game basis. Counting points motivates and gives performance feedback. If both players have good concentration and prefer not to keep score, that is fine.

In these games the winner must have ten points and win by a margin of at least two points. If the score is tied at 9–9, they continue play until one of the players is at least two points ahead (11–9, 15–13, etc.). Players change sides every four games.

Drill **86**

TWO-PLAYER DOUBLES— TEN-POINT GAME

This is an especially valuable drill since it develops doubles skills yet requires only two players. The drill should be an integral part of the practice procedures of all players. It is, perhaps, the best drill for developing doubles skills, and in some respects it is more valuable than practicing the game of doubles itself. The drill forces a player to develop singles skills also (return of service and serve and volley). Two separate drills can take place on each court at the same time if there is a shortage of courts.

Partners play crosscourt points using half of the doubles court. The playing area is surrounded by the net, the doubles sideline, the baseline, and the center service line (with an imaginary continuation of it to the baseline). One of the players serves a complete ten-point game, then the partner serves a game. The drill should be practiced in the forehand court, as well as the backhand court (Fig. 86.A). If a player is a member of an established doubles team, playing one particular side regularly, then all practice serving should be directed to that same service court. The server should follow his serve to the net.

Fig. 86   Playing crosscourt doubles points.

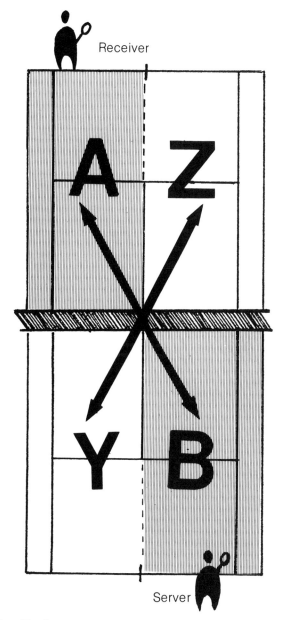

86A   Playing crosscourt points from deuce court (A to B). Points can also be played in the ad court (Y to Z). Begin points with service.

RECEIVER FOLLOWS HIS RETURN TO NET

This drill requires the receiver to follow each service to net to develop an aggressive return. He can either take the serve early, hit while moving slowly forward, or use the slow crosscourt dink return of service to get to the net as quickly as the server. Now and then the opportunity to use the lob volley over the server's head presents itself. Ten-point games are played, and the drill is done in both the deuce and ad courts.

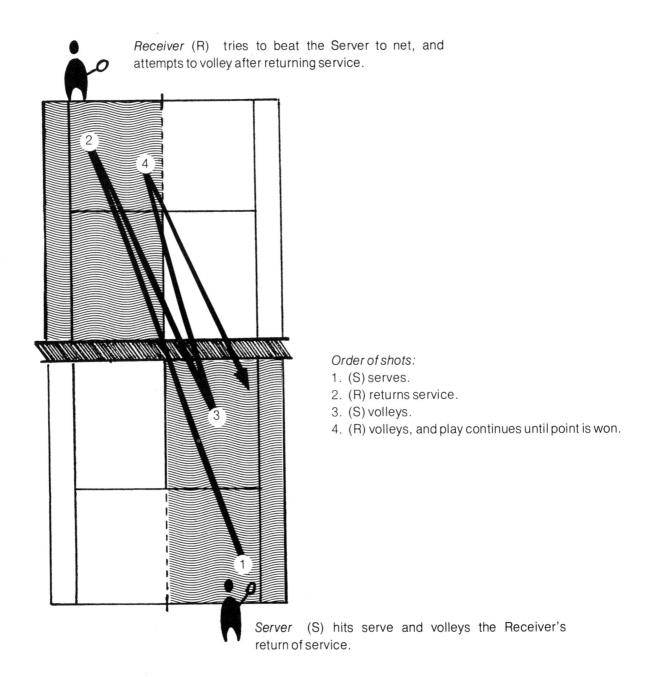

Receiver (R) tries to beat the Server to net, and attempts to volley after returning service.

Order of shots:
1. (S) serves.
2. (R) returns service.
3. (S) volleys.
4. (R) volleys, and play continues until point is won.

Server (S) hits serve and volleys the Receiver's return of service.

86B   Receiver follows return of service to net.

Drill **87**

SERVE AND VOLLEY— TEN-POINT GAME

Many fine clay-court tournament players rarely come to the net and, as a result, are largely ineffective when playing fast courts or those which have bad bounces (grass). This drill is designed to develop a net game.

One player simply serves and follows his serve to the net for the entire ten-point game, then the partner does the same. The server should rush toward the net as quickly as possible in order to avoid making low and half volleys.

Drill 88

SECOND SERVICE— TEN-POINT GAME

In this drill the server is allowed only one service instead of the usual two, while he and his partner play a ten-point game. The second serve is used exclusively to develop reliability. This drill will expose an erratic second service and make it indelibly clear that consistency must be improved. (You may wish to refer to "Drills for Intermediates" 48–51.) This exercise amounts to concentrated second-service practice. When a player does the drill successfully, with practically no faults and with reasonable pace, his confidence will be bolstered. With a reliable second service he can afford to take more risks in a match with a powerful first service placed close to the lines.

Drill

NO SERVE—
TEN-POINT GAME

This drill is excellent for players confined to fast court surfaces who seldom engage in backcourt rallies. It is designed to develop the baseline game, and it is also a good conditioner since the points are lengthy. Two players stand behind their baselines, and whoever has the ball bounces and strokes it deep down the middle of the opposite court at two-thirds speed. The partner returns the ball anyplace in the singles court in an effort to win the point. He can drive, slice, or dropshot, and he can remain in the backcourt or come to the net behind the ball. There must be one groundstroke executed by each player before a volley attempt. In other words, the player who puts the ball in play to start the point cannot follow the ball to net. Concentrate on hitting solid groundstrokes that land between the service and baselines, and minimize risk by keeping the balls away from the lines.

Drill **90**

PLACEMENT-ERROR TALLY —TEN-POINT GAME

Fig. 90.1 Simple Tennis Error-Placement Analysis Chart

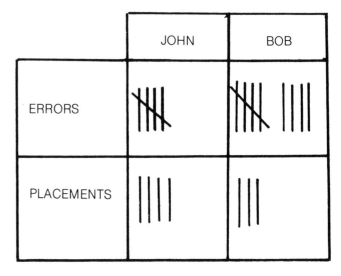

In this drill, two play a no-serve ten-point game identical to previous Drill 89 while a third person records all errors and placements. A placement is an outright winning shot or a ball which is impossible to return. After seeing your log of placements in relation to errors, you will have a better knowledge of your offense and defense (Fig. 90.1).

For a more detailed and accurate analysis of your weaknesses and strengths, you can use the second chart (Fig. 90.2). This chart is especially beneficial to tournament players.

A player who makes too many errors is probably overhitting. This means a player is not performing within his capabilities because of swinging too hard or going too close to the lines or net. A player who rarely makes placements and allows his opponent many winners is likely playing too defensively, limiting his potential for improvement. However there are some players who should favor either offense or defense in their development.

WHO SHOULD STRESS DEFENSE?

The fast and mobile player who has stamina, determination, and patience has excellent defensive potential. The player who is going to spend most of his tennis career playing on slow clay courts should definitely develop a tough defense. The player who is a newcomer to the game and wants quick success in competitive play should stress defense. A careful, retrieving-type player makes more rapid improvement in the early stages of tennis development than the hitter. Although the defensive player can achieve tournament success, he can never become a great player without heavy artillery.

WHO SHOULD STRESS OFFENSE?

If you are slow afoot then definitely plan to stroke with pace. The harder you hit the less you have to run. Several top players have only average speed afoot but have tremendous power with placement. Most great players have controlled power *and* speed of foot. Controlled power is the name of the world-class game. The ideal setting for offensive power is a fast court (grass, wood, or fast cement) and hard and light balls. Many California tournaments are played under conditions that encourage the use of power by serving and volleying and stroking balls on the rise.

Fig. 90.2 Detailed Tennis Error-Placement Analysis Chart

This chart can also be divided, according to the needs of the players concerned, into separate categories for drop shots, half volleys, returns of service, drives and slices. Percentages of first serves in play can also be listed, as can service breaks.

Name of Player_____Name of Opponent_____Date _____

Name of Winner_____Score _____

	ERROR Beyond Baseline	ERROR Into Net	ERROR Wide of Sideline	PLACEMENT
Forehand Groundstroke				
Backhand Groundstroke				
Forehand Volley				
Backhand Volley				
Overhead				
Forehand Lob				
Backhand Lob				
First Service				(Aces)
Second Service	(Double Fault)	(Double Fault)	(Double Fault)	(Aces)

Drill 91

SHORT-BALL PUTAWAY AND DROP SHOT— TEN-POINT GAME

The ability to put away a short, soft ball for an outright winner is an important asset, typifying an international-class tournament player. If you lack the power, consistency, or confidence to hit the opponent's short ball out of his reach, this drill will help you. Most players find the forehand side has the most potential for this putaway shot.

The ball is put in play by one of the players at two-thirds speed down the middle of the court, and the players play out the point using only groundstrokes. No volleying is allowed. By hitting deep to the corners, partners attempt to extract the short ball from each other, so that they can either put it away cleanly or dropshot for a winner. If an outright winner occurs either way, the hitter is awarded two points instead of one. The player receives one point for an opponent's error. A ten-point game is played.

Drill 92

BACKCOURT— TEN-POINT GAME

You can attain depth of shot either by hitting hard, which can be risky, or stroking balls high over the net. On backcourt points it is better to err a little over the baseline than to miss by hitting the ball into the net.

In this drill you play backcourt points, hitting only groundstrokes that must land between your partner's service and baselines. The hitter loses the point if his ball lands in either of his partner's service boxes. To start the point, either player bounces and strokes the ball at two-thirds speed deep down the middle of the court. The point is then played out, and a ten-point game is played (Fig. 92). This short-ball penalty game may also be played by using a service to start the points. Try to stroke the ball with good pace and depth, but do not take risks by going too close to the lines.

ADVANTAGES OF DEPTH

There are six big advantages of depth:

(1) By keeping an opponent behind his baseline, you have more time to get to his drives and drop shots.
(2) By keeping the balls deep, you lessen the opponent's ability to hit wide and angled shots.
(3) When the opponent is forced to hit from behind his baseline, it is more difficult for him to advance to the net and attack.
(4) By keeping the balls deep to your opponent, you have a better chance of extracting a short ball that you can attack.
(5) Balls hit deeply to an opponent are more likely to draw errors than short balls (near the service line) because he has less time to react and prepare the return. A ball loses approximately 50 percent of its speed after bouncing, therefore the longer the ball travels through the air before bouncing, the faster it reaches the opponent.
(6) An extremely deep ball is more likely to cause an opponent to miss because there is a greater likelihood he will have to move backward than forward to return the ball, resulting in a defensive shot lacking in power and accuracy.

Fig. 92 Backcourt ten-point game.

Partners exchange groundstrokes. Balls must land between the service and baselines or they lose the point.

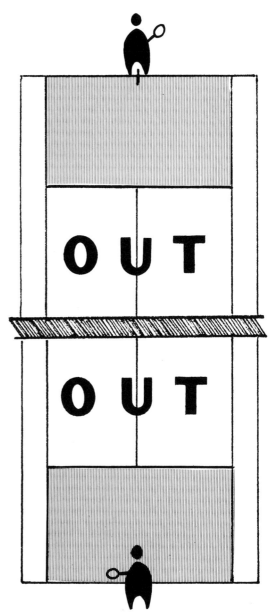

Drill **93**

HALF BACKCOURT— TEN-POINT GAME

This is identical with Drill 92, except you hit into only one half of the backcourt area. Before each game you and your partner decide which half of each other's backcourt you will hit into. You have four choices: going down the line with your forehand to your partner's backhand; going down the line with your backhand to your partner's forehand; stroking crosscourt forehands; or hitting backhands crosscourt (Fig. 93). This drill breaks down depth stroking to reveal specific strengths and weaknesses. The results of this drill might surprise you.

Fig. 93   Half-backcourt ten-point game.

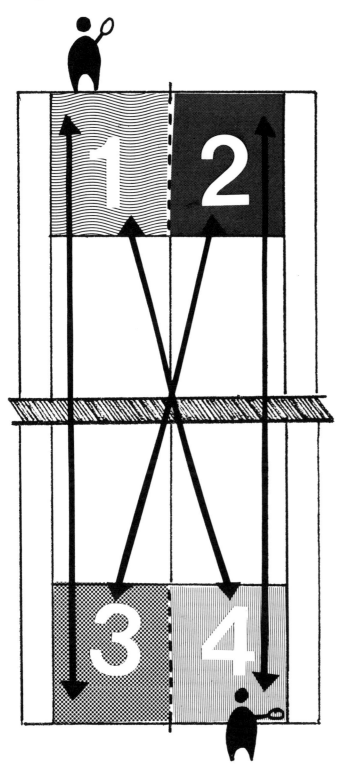

Partners play ten-point groundstroke games using any of the following combinations for one complete game: 1 to 4—forehands only; 2 to 3—backhands only; 1 to 3 and 2 to 4—one player using the forehand and the other the backhand. If the ball lands outside of the designated area it is a miss.

SECTION V

APPENDIX

OFF-COURT DRILLS

RAINY-DAY DRILLS

These drills do not have to be performed on a court and are excellent to use in inclement weather. Many can be done in the cellar of a home or an apartment building. The inside of an empty garage can be utilized.

The following drills and exercises enable players of all levels to develop their games seven days a week, and 365 days a year. They do not require a large indoor backboard area.

Beginning Drills

1, 2, 3, 4, 5, 6, 7, 8, 9, 10, 12, 14, 21, 22

Intermediate Drills

24, 25, 30, 31, 32, 33, 34, 35, 37, 38, 44, 50, 53

Advanced and Tournament-Level Drills

54, 55, 64

DRILLS TO USE WHEN A COURT IS UNAVAILABLE

These exercises do not require a tennis court and can be done in a driveway, school yard, or even a parking lot. A few can even be done in your living room.

Beginning Drills

1, 2, 3, 4, 5, 6, 7, 8, 9, 10, 11, 12, 13, 14, 15, 17, 18 (Pavement or Driveway Rallying), 20, 21, 22, 23 (Serving to Fence)

Intermediate Drills

24, 25, 26, 27, 30, 31, 32, 33, 34, 35, 37, 38, 39 (Smashing to Fence from Self-Tossed Ball), 44, 50, 51, 53

Advanced and Tournament-Level Drills

54, 55, 56 (Solo and Shadow Tennis in Park or Lot), 64

BACKBOARD DRILLS

These drills are listed separately in order for you to have a quick reference for practice on a backboard or wall. Backboard practice is an excellent method of grooving strokes. A desirable wall should be smooth, and the adjacent ground should be flat and preferably paved so true bounces will occur.

Twenty to thirty feet of stroking space from the backboard is necessary for groundstrokes, however most volley drills can be executed within fifteen feet of a backboard. All of the "Rainy-Day Drills," as well as those listed as "Drills to Use When a Court Is Unavailable," can be performed at a backboard facility. The following are the backboard drills:

Beginning Drills
16
Intermediate Drills
28, 40, 41, 44, 45, 46, 47, 48, 51, 52
Advanced and Tournament-Level Drills
65, 66, 67, 68, 78

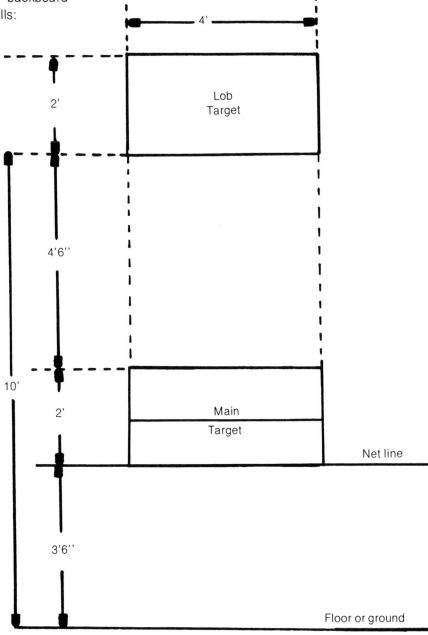

BACKBOARD DIAGRAM

Backboard Illustration (The lower half of the Main Target is for passing shot and dropshot practice)

GLOSSARY

These are the author's definitions of terms. To learn the specific names of the tennis court areas and lines, refer to the diagram on page 223.

Descriptions of drills and exercises used in this book are explained from a right-hander's position. Left-handers will apply the information accordingly.

Ad court. The Left service court, or the service box on your left side as you face the net. The term *ad court* is derived from the score, meaning one of the players has the advantage (*ad*) in score when a point is started in this court; the score will always be odd.

All-court game. The ability to execute sound strokes from any part of the court, without any particular stroke weakness.

Angled volley or shot. A stroked ball which draws an opponent beyond the sideline of the court. The best angled shots are directed crosscourt, and made from as close to the net as possible.

Approach shot. An offensive ground stroke that is followed to net. A player usually approaches the net, or hits an approach shot off an opponent's short, slow ball.

Backboard. A smooth wall, or similar structure, from which the ball rebounds with enough power and consistency to enable a person to maintain a rally.

Backcourt. The area between the service and base-lines where most advanced volleys and ground-strokes should land.

Backspin. See **Underspin**.

Backswing. Moving the racket in a backward direction to prepare for its forward movement. It is the first part of a stroke or serve, and is followed by the forward swing.

Baseliner or baseline player. A player who hits the vast majority of his shots as groundstrokes, instead of volleying. Most of his balls are hit from just behind the baseline.

Change of pace. Stroking the ball at different speeds in order to upset the timing of an opponent.

Crosscourt. A ball directed diagonally across the court, not parallel with the sidelines. For example, right-handers hitting forehands to each other would be rallying toward each other's corners in a crosscourt manner.

Depth. A served ball landing just inside the opponent's service line, or one which lands between the service line and the baseline during play. In top tournament tennis *good depth* means a ball landing no further than nine or ten feet from the opponent's baseline.

Deuce court. The right service court, or the service box on your right side as you face the net. The term *deuce court* is derived from the score, meaning the total number of points played in the game is always even when a point is started in this court.

Dink. A low, soft ball, usually hit when the opponent is at the net, and in this case not intended to be an outright winner. It can also be used with the opponent in the backcourt, when a player does not want to risk a drop shot by going too close to the lines or net.

Down-the-line. A ball hit parallel with, and reasonably close to, a sideline.

Drills. Carefully planned activities that lead toward improvement in tennis, and do not include the playing of regularly scored matches. Usually referring to advanced rally sustaining procedures, however often used synonymously with the word *exercises* in this book.

Drive. Offensive backcourt stroke hit with a full swing off forehand or backhand. Referring to a ball hit with slight overspin, rather than the underspin of the slice. A drive can also be flat; however, this author does not recommend it.

Drop shot. A soft ball, with pronounced backspin, hit barely over the net to produce an outright winner or an error. Preferably hit from inside the baseline and directed near the opponent's sideline.

Drop volley. The same meaning as *touch volley* or *stop volley*. A volleyed ball hit softly, low, and near the net to produce an outright winner or error.

Exercises. Carefully planned activities that lead toward improvement in tennis, and do not include the playing of regularly scored matches. Most often used synonymously with the word *drills* in this book.

Follow-through. The completion of the swing after the racket strings have left the ball.

Foot fault. A service fault, most often caused by stepping on the baseline, or in the court, while striking the ball. It can also be called when the player takes a walking or running motion before the service delivery.

Forecourt. The area between the service line and the net where a player tries to do most of his volleying or smashing.

Forward swing. The act of bringing the racket forward and toward the net before and during contact, and after the ball is struck. The backswing is the first part of the stroke or serve.

Grooving. The process of learning a stroke to such an extent that thought about its various components is not necessary in execution. When a player is grooving his shots he is attempting to overlearn them.

Groundstroke. A stroke that is made with either forehand or backhand, after the ball hits the ground. Groundstrokes include drives, slices, loops, dinks, drop shots, and half volleys.

Half volley. A stroke in which the racket contacts the ball immediately after it touches the ground. It is a member of the groundstroke family and a misnomer, as it is not a partial volley. It could be termed a quick pickup.

Hit. When the racket makes contact with the ball at any time.

Hitting deep. Hitting a ball near the baseline of the opponent's court so that he cannot easily make an offensive shot from it.

Hitting short or shallow. Hitting a ball that lands near the net, in the center of the opponent's court. It is often a soft ball that can be easily attacked.

Inside of baseline or service line. A point about a foot or two from the baseline or service line between the line and the net.

Lob. A groundstroked ball hit high in the air that can be either an offensive or defensive shot.

Loop. A groundstroked ball that is hit with a high trajectory rather than directly toward the opponent's court. It usually reaches a height of ten or eleven feet, and is slightly lower than the offensive lob. If it can be done with accuracy, it is desirable to stroke the loop with overspin.

Match. A tennis contest using official scoring and regulation match procedures in the playing of points, games, and sets.

On the fly. Hitting a ball before it touches the ground. A volley is a ball hit on the fly.

Overhead. A stroke hit directly overhead with a compact service motion. It is the answer to a lob and can either be taken on the fly or allowed to bounce. Also called an overhand smash or smash.

Overlearn. To master a stroke so thoroughly that it can be performed as a whole, without thought for its individual components. An overlearned stroke can also be referred to as *deeply grooved*.

Overspin. The ball's motion, in which the top part of the ball is spinning away from the hitter. After striking the ground the overspin ball jumps slightly forward and therefore has considerable offensive potential. Groundstrokes and serves are often hit with overspin. *Overspin* and *topspin* mean the same thing.

Pace. The speed of the ball—fast is desirable. Top players hit with excellent pace.

Placement. (a) An outright winner, or unreturnable ball, that a player cannot touch, or barely reaches with his racket. (b) Directing a ball to a place on the court that the hitter aims for. Good placement means fine control.

Rally. Stroking the ball back and forth over the net either in match play or while drilling. A long rally means many consecutive balls hit with either volleys, or ground strokes.

Range of correctness. The principle that there is more than one specific grip or method used to properly stroke a tennis ball. For example, there are three forehand grips that a great game can be based upon: Eastern, Australian, and Midwestern (between Eastern and Western). There are grips out of the range of correctness that handicap a tournament player, such as a Western service grip, or an extreme backhand grip for volleying.

Ranked player. An outstanding tournament player who is given the honor of a numerical rating for the previous year's play. The player with the best record is number one, the second best is number two, etc.

Retriever. A defensive player primarily concerned with simply returning the ball rather than placing an opponent at a disadvantage. His strategy is based upon an opponent missing the shot, rather than making a winner, or powerful placement.

Short ball. A ball that can be easily attacked by landing too close to the net and not close enough to the baseline. As the standard of play becomes better, greater depth of shot is necessary. Occasionally, a well-placed short ball landing near a sideline is an excellent tactical play.

Shot. The end result of hitting any ball except a service.

Slice. A particular spin placed on a ball. A ground stroke or volley hit with the lower edge of the racket leading. A sliced ground stroke has underspin and a little sidespin. The forward path of the racket creates an angle of less than forty-five degrees to the ground. On the service, *slice* means sidespin that could pull the receiver to his right.

Smash. Same as overhead or overhead smash.

Stroke. The act of hitting the ball. It is often used synonymously with *form*, and usually refers to ground strokes and volleys.

Topspin. See **Overspin**.

Touch. Implies control and ability to make delicate shots such as soft, angled returns, drop shots, and drop volleys. It is like a player touching the ball with his hand, rather than hitting it with a racket. It is also the ability to be effective without using great ball speed.

Twist. In this text, it is used synonymously with *American Twist*. A served ball hit with overspin and sidespin, resulting in a high-bouncing ball, that breaks to an opponent's backhand after hitting the ground. It is a safe serve and often makes a fine second service. There is also a reverse twist which the author does not recommend.

Underspin. The ball's motion in which the top part of the ball is spinning toward the hitter. After striking the ground the ball stays low and does not hop forward with speed. On a great drop shot the ball hardly goes forward at all. *Underspin* and *backspin* have the same meaning.

Volley. A stroke used to hit the ball before it bounces. It includes the sidearmed shots but not overheads.

Wall. See **Backboard**.

TENNIS COURT DIAGRAM

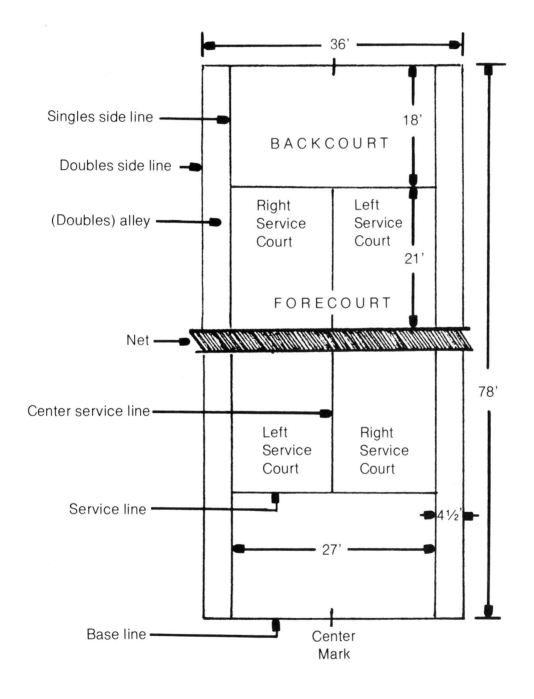

Singles side line

Doubles side line

(Doubles) alley

36'

BACKCOURT

18'

Right Service Court

Left Service Court

21'

FORECOURT

Net

78'

Center service line

Left Service Court

Right Service Court

Service line

4½'

27'

Base line

Center Mark